Contents

KU-254-081

Walkers and the Law; Global Positioning System (GPS); Visitors and the Mountain Environment; Safety on the Hills; Glossary of Gaelic Names; Useful Organisations; Ordnance Survey Maps

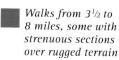

Short walks from 1½ to 6 miles with some modest uphill walking

Walks from 3½ to 8 miles, some with strenuous sections over rugged terrain

Demanding walks from 6½ to 18 miles over rugged terrain with some stiff climbs in remote country

Dalfaber

Aviemore

1465

Meall
a' Bhuachaille
2654

Glenmore Forest Park
The Queen's Forest

6
19
23
26
27

18
Boat of Garten
Coylumbridge
GLEN
MORE
Glenmore
12
Rothiemurchus

Morlich

2435
Stac na
h-Iolaire

24

20

Bynack
More
3574

Carn
Eilrig
2435

Castle
Hill
2366

CAIRN GORM
4084

CAIRN GORM

2932

Sgòran
Dubh Mòr
3635

CAIRNGORM

Lairig
Ghru

Shelter
Stone
3983

Loch
Avon

Beinn
a' Chaorainn
3553

3924

BEN AVON
3843

GRAMPIAN MOUN

Braeriach

4248

4296

MOUNTAINS

Carn Eas
3556

Creag an
Dail Bheag
2830

3658

Loch
Einich
4149

Sgòr
Gaoith

BEN MACDUI

4236

3788

Derry
Cairngorm
3789

3051

Beinn
Bhreac

Carn na
Drochaide
2681

Cairn Toul

3303

The Devil's
Point

3329

Carn
a' Mhaim

Monadh
Mòr
3651

Beinn
Bhrotain
3795

Sgòr Mòr
2667

Glen
Lui

Creag
Bhalg

Mar
Lodge

Allanaquoich

Braemar
Castle

21

15

Muir Cottage

Muir

Inverey

FOREST OF

Auchallater

2819

The Colonel's
Bed

Cairn Geldie
2039

Glen Ey
Burn

Baddoch

Creag nan
Gabhar
2736

3276

Carn an Fhidhleir
or Carn Ealar

2204

Geldie
Burn

3300
An Sgarsoch

Carn
Liath
2676

Bynack
Burn

Carn
Bhac
3014

3098

2989

Sgòr Mòr
2906

3340

2605

An Socach
3073

Beinn
Iutharn Mhòr
3424

Carn
a' Gheòidh
3194

3059

Loch
Vrotachan

2882
Braigh
Sròn Ghorm

Gleann
Dirìdh

3377

Carn an Righ

3504

THE
CAIRNWELL

Devil's
Elbow

Glas Maol
Caenl

3238

3159

Glas
Tulaichean
3449

Forest
Lodge

Loch
Loch

River Tilt

Glen
Loch

2377

Creag
Leacach

BEINN A' GHLO

3673

Gleann Fearnach

Dalmunzie
House
Hotel

Ben Gulabin
2641

2470
Carn
an Daimh

Gleann Mòr

3201

Carn Liath

2962

Ben
Vuirich

Meall a' Choire
Bhuidhe
2846

Spittal of
Glenshee

2632
Ben Earb

2600
Meall
Uaine

Meaina Letter or
Duchray Hill
2301

Loch
Valigan

Gleann Mòr

Glen Tilt

14

Bridge
of Tilt

Allt Glen
Loch

Loch
Moraig

Creag an t-
Sìthean

Dalnaglar
Castle

Blair
Atholl

Bonskeid
House

Little House

2092

Cray
Mount
Blair

1879
Lamh
Dearg

Pass of
Killiecrankie

Creag Dhubh

Balvarran

Ashintully
Castle

Brewland

Moulin

Kirkmichael

Blacklunans

SCALE 1:250 000 or 1 INCH to 4 MILES 1CM to 2.5KM

KILOMETRES 0 2½ 5 10 15

MILES 0 2 4 6 8 10

KEYMAP HEIGHTS SHOWN IN FEET

arrow 2598

Kirkton of
Glenbuchat

Castle
Castle   Mains of
Kildrummy
A97

The Socach
2356   Breagach
Hill   Bellabeg
1825   Forbestown   Glenkindie   Glenbuchat
Castle   Sinnahard
Carn   2600   Glen Ernan   Strathdon   Glenbuchat
Ealasaid   Invereman   Castle   Towie
House   Heugh-head   Miltown
of Towie
Geal Charn   A944   Waterside   Boultenstone
2207   Candacraig   Frosty
House   Hill

Cock   Colnabaichin   Craig of   Hillockhead   1557
Bridge   Corgarff   Bunzeach
Castle   Tornahaish   A97
Delnadamph

2310   2294   Mona Gowan   Logie   Migvie   East
2456   Coldstone   Davoch
Carn Leac   Coynach
2633   Saighaer   2442   2861   Tarland
2721   Brown Cow   Brigdefoot   Leys   B9119
Hill   Ordie

AINS   River Gairn   Gairnshiel   Peter's Hill   Culblean   Glendavan
Lodge   1863   Hill   House
B976   Lary   1983
Glen Gairn   Candacraig   Dinnet

Gleallaig   2438   Bridge   3   Milton of   22
Hill   Collacriech   Culsh   of Ga   9   Tullich
Bush   Greystone
Crathie   Abergeldie   BALLATER   Glen Tanar
Balmoral   Castle   Littlemill   B976   Pannanich   House
Castle   Crathie   Hill   Black   1742
Balnault   Mains of   Bridge of Muick   Craig   Glen
Inver   Abergeldie   House of
Invergelder   Easter   Birkhall   Glenmuick   Forest of Glen Tanar
Balmoral
Ballachlaggan   2058
R   Creag   The Coyles   1956   Cairn   Clachan Yell
nan Gall   of Muick   2293   2081
Forest   1969   Aucholzie   Leuchan   Cock Cairn
2387

Glen Muick   2289   3080
Balmoral Forest   MOUNT KEEN   Hill   2141
2827   2365   Hill of
LOCHNAGAR   Conachcraig   Fashéilach   Saughs
3791   Spittal of   17   2162
White Mount   Glenmuick   28
Cairn   Dubh
Bannoch   Loch   Glas-allt-Shiel   Black Hill   Water of Mark   Glen Mark
3314   of Mark   Easter
3268   Broad   Balloch   Glen Lee   2276   Invermark
Cairn   2731   Monawee   Lodge   Auchronie
3143   Loch   Tarfs
Tolmount   Esk   2726   Water of Unich   Glenlee   Loch Lee
Inchgrundle   Glen Effock
Glen Doll   2815   Lair of
2954   Glendoll   Aldararie   Muckle   2424   2273
Finalty   Lodge   Cairn   2699   Cruys   West Knock
Hill   3043   Braedownie   Ben Tirran
Mayar   3108   Loch
Driesh   Brandy   2941   2544   Hunthill
White Hill   2260   Lodge
2302   Clova   1759
2483   Hill of
Cairn Inks   2410   Berran
2256   2129   Wheen   2478
Cairn   Cairn   Finbracks
Baddoch   of Barns   2381   Hill of
2428   1915   Glansie   1900
The Drums   Hill of
Badandun   2228   Garbet
Hill   1992   1799   Clachnabrain   1788   Peat
Eskielawn   1998   Auld Darkney   1682   Hill
Glenprosen   1676   Pinderachy
Village   Hill of   Glenmoy   Auchnacree
Coutdrnach   970
Glenarm   Redheugh   Glenogi   Deuchar   1031
Glenquiech   Hill   Tullo
Kirkton of   Glenhead Farm   Easter   Ogil   Hill   Fern
Glenisla   Lednathie   Hornenaugh   Newmill   Noranside
Backwater   Longdrum   of Insheawan   Deuchar
Reservoir   2022   Dykehead   Burnside
B951   Bellaty   1630   Cat Law   Pearsie

Keymap 2

SCALE 1:250 000 or 1 INCH to 4 MILES *1CM to 2.5KM*

KILOMETRES
0   2   4   6   8   10   15

MILES
0   2   4   6   8   10

KEYMAP HEIGHTS SHOWN IN FEET

North Kessock
Longman Point
Balloch
Culloden Forest
Newton
Cantraywood
Dalcross
Castle
Easter Galcantray
Achindown
Kirkton of Barevan
Mains of Clava
Bruachmary
of Wood

INVERNESS
Culloden
Cantraydoune

Smithton
Culloden Muir
1746

Culcabock
Westhill
Leys Castle
House of Daviot
Casbletown
Carn Sgumain 1370
Banchor
Dulsie
River Findhorn

A9
Beinn Bhuidhe Mhòr 1799
Drynachan Lodge
Streens

Essich
Davict
Craggie
2016
Carn nan Tri-tighearnan
Daless

Scatraig
Beinn Bhreac 1675
Moy Burn
Meall a' Bhreacraibh 1809
Loch Moy

Balnatoich
Meall Mór 1611
Moy Hall
Ruthven

Tombreck
Moy
Carn an t-Sean-liathanach 2076

Farr
Carn na h-Easgainn 2022
Balvraid

Farr House
Tomatin Distillery
Inverbrough
Carn à' Choire Mhòir 2057
Carn Glas choire
2162

Brinmore
Beinn Bhreac 1969
Tomatin
Findhorn Bridge
Kyllachy House
Carn nam Bain-tighearna 1333

East Croachy
2071
Corrievorrie
Slochd
2082

Carn na Saobhaidh 2321
Glen Kyllachy
Dalmigave Lodge
Carn Phris Mhòir 2021
Invertaidnan
A9
13
Lochanhu

2637
Beinn Bhreac Mhòr
Glen Mazeran
Carn Dubh 'Ic an Deòir
2461
Dalnahaitnach
Carrbridge
B9153

Carn Ghriogair 2647
Dalmigavie
Carn Sleamhuinn 2217
Beinn Ghuilbin 1895
Ki
4

Coignafearn Lodge
Avielochan
Granish
Daltaber
1465

Dalbeg Forest
Calpa Mór 2668
Carn Coire na h-Easgainn 2591
2444 Cnoc Fraing
Aviemore
Boylumbre
6

MOUNTAINS
2652
2703 Geal-charn Mór
Craigellachie
19

ADHLIATH
Carn Sgulain 2665
Doune
23
26
iemore

2879
Carn an Fhreiceadain
2365
An Suidhe 1775
Alvie
27

3015
A' Chailleach 3045
Raitts
Speybank
Kincraig
Inverashie House
Feshiebridge

Carn Bàn 3087
Creag an Lòin 1788
Lynchat
7
25
Farr
Balnespick
Insh
Inshriach Forest
Sgòran Dubh Mór 3635

Carn Dearg
KINGUSSIE
A9
Loch Insh

2
Newtonmore
Ruthven
Ruthven Barracks
Drumguish
10
Auchlean
3443 Carn Bàn Mór
3658

A86
Glen Banchor
Creag Dhubh
Glentromie Lodge
Glentruim House
Glen Feshie
Sgòr Gaoith
3268

731
dalgowan
Glentruim House
Creag nam Bodach 1610
2058 Meall Buidhe
Lynaberack Lodge
Glenfeshie Lodge
Mullach 3338

Cluny Castle

Keymap 2

At-a-glance...

Walk	Page	Start	Nat. Grid Reference	Distance	Height Gain	Time
Boat of Garten	20	Boat of Garten	NH 936189	4 miles (6.2km)	160ft (50m)	2 hrs
The Braes of Abernethy	22	Dorback Lodge	NJ 077168	4¼ miles (6.8km)	460ft (140m)	2½ hrs
Bynack More from Glenmore	73	Allt Mor car park	NH 983087	14¼ miles (23km)	2,625ft (800m)	7½ hrs
Cambus o' May and the Muir of Dinnet	66	Dinnet	NO 459987	9¼ miles (14.9km)	445ft (135m)	4½ hrs
Carn an Fhreiceadain	76	Kingussie	NH 755007	10½ miles (17km)	2,280ft (695m)	5½ hrs
Carn Daimh from Glenlivet	48	Tomnavoulin	NJ 208265	6½ miles (10.5km)	1,150ft (350m)	3½ hrs
Carrbridge and General Wade's Rd.	39	Carrbridge	NH 907227	7¾ miles (12.3km)	625ft (190m)	4 hrs
Craigendarroch	18	Ballater	NO 365960	1½ miles (2.4km)	640ft (195m)	1½ hrs
Creag a Chalamain and Castle Hill	37	Allt Mor car park	NH 983087	8 miles (12.8km)	1,605ft (490m)	4½ hrs
Creag Bheag and Loch Gynack	26	Kingussie	NH 755007	4¼ miles (6.7km)	835ft (255m)	2½ hrs
Eag a' Chait and Loch Morlich	54	West end of Loch Morlich	NH 956097	7¾ miles (12.3km)	1,015ft (310m)	4 hrs
Fiacaill and Cairn Lochan	60	Coire Cas car park	NH 989061	6½ miles (10.5km)	2,625ft (800m)	5 hrs
Five Bridges Walk, Ballater	30	Ballater	NO 369957	5½ miles (8.7km)	115ft (35m)	2½ hrs
Gleann Eanaich	70	Whitewell	NH 914090	13 miles (20.8km)	985ft (300m)	6½ hrs
Glen Banchor and Craggan	16	Glen Road, Newtonmore	NN 715991	3 miles (4.75km)	345ft (105m)	1½ hrs
Glen Brown and Tom nam Marbh	28	White Bridge	NJ 133209	4½ miles (7.3km)	785ft (240m)	2½ hrs
Glen Feshie	33	Near Achlean, Glen Feshie	NN 850985	3½ miles (5.5km)	415ft (125m)	2 hrs
Glen Lui and Derry Lodge	45	Linn of Dee car park	NO 063898	7 miles (11.1km)	330ft (100m)	3½ hrs
Glen Tilt	42	Blair Atholl	NN 874662	6 miles (9.4km)	150ft (50m)	3 hrs
Grantown-on-Spey	35	Grantown-on-Spey	NJ 034280	7 miles (11.1km)	115ft (35m)	3½ hrs
The Lairig Ghru	83	Whitewell	NH 914090	12¾ miles (20.5km)	1,705ft (520m)	7 hrs
The Lily Loch and Loch an Eilein	24	Inverdruie	NH 901110	6 miles (9.7km)	445ft (135m)	3 hrs
Loch an Eilein	57	Coylum Bridge	NH 914106	8 miles (12.9km)	425ft (130m)	4 hrs
Loch Garten and Loch Mallachie	14	2 miles east of Boat of Garten	NH 971185	1¾ miles (2.75km)	N/a	1 hr
Loch Muick	51	Spittal of Glenmuick	NO 309851	7½ miles (12km)	230ft (70m)	3½ hrs
Lochnagar and Loch Muick	86	Spittal of Glenmuick	NO 309851	14 miles (22.4km)	2,790ft (850m)	8 hrs
Morrone	63	The Duck Pond, Braemar	NO 143910	7 miles (11.3km)	2,015ft (615m)	4 hrs
Sron na Lairige and Braeriach	79	Loch an Eilein	NH 897085	18 miles (28.9km)	3,410ft (1,040m)	10 hrs

Comments

From the peaceful village of Boat of Garten this well-signed walk passes through pine woods and farmland to return by the Spey, with the chance to spot an osprey.

Waterproof footwear is recommended on this walk which involves fording quite a few streams. It goes nowhere in particular but returns through sand dunes — unique in an inland walk.

This is a strenuous and demanding route which should be attempted only if the weather is good. Be prepared for rough walking over path and moorland. The views from the summit reward the effort.

The shallow lochs of Kinord and Davan at the start of this walk are rich in birdlife. They are followed by the pine and birch forests on Culblean Hill and the wooded banks of the River Dee.

The Monadhliath Mountains are part of the southern Grampians and face the Cairngorms across the Spey valley. The summit of Carn an Fhreiceadain gives fine views and a flavour of these desolate hills.

A walk on the Glenlivet Estate, climbing up through woodland and open country to the summit of Carn Daimh. It then drops back down with spectacular views across the glen.

Sluggan Bridge is a memorable beauty spot reached by part of General Wade's Road. The path can be wet and there is a stream to ford, so take waterproof footwear or be prepared to wade barefoot.

The climb starts in delightful woodland where red squirrels are common. The summit looks to Lochnagar in the south-west, a view best seen in the low light of early morning or late summer evening.

The opening section of this walk takes advantage of newly-constructed and restored paths before reaching hill terrain. Beautiful woodland and forest paths are included for a delightful route.

Creag Bheag is an outstanding viewpoint for Strathspey, while the way back to Kingussie is along a path following the shore of Loch Gynack.

The highlights of this walk are the pass of Eag a' Chait with its grand views to the summits of the Cairngorms, and the ancient pine forest complete with reindeer.

Walk or take the chairlift for the first part of this route, then head for the rim of Coire an t-Sneachda corrie and the summit of Cairn Lochan.

Ballater's Victorian heyday is remembered in the magnificent station and several military memorials along this walk which passes through woods and criss-crosses the River Dee and its tributaries.

Gleann Eanaich is one of the finest of the Cairngorm glens, replete with red deer. This walk follows the burn right through its heart to the beautiful Loch Eanaich at its head.

Taken on a fine summer evening, this walk to Craggan offers views over the Spey valley to the Cairngorms beyond. It returns to the village of Newtonmore beside the waters of the River Calder.

On part of the Glenlivet Estate, this route is not accessible during the deer stalking season, but otherwise provides pleasant walking through open country with some woodland and waterside scenery.

Follow the path to one of the most beautiful waterfalls in the Cairngorms, set amongst pine trees below the peak of Carn Bàn Beag and above the calm of Glen Feshie.

This route affords fine views over Glen Lui to Derry Cairngorm and Ben Macdui, the second highest mountain in Britain. The walk is not suitable for younger children.

A fine glacial valley, this walk sets off from the historic home of the Dukes of Atholl for a circuit of the lower reaches of the glen amid stunning mountain scenery.

A gentle walk along the banks of the Spey, famous for its salmon, starts off through attractive woodland and finishes on one of General Wade's military roads.

A good walk for fine summer weather when the three passes of Lairig Ghru, the Chalamain Gap and Eag a' Chait should be free from snow. It also takes in the Rothiemurchus pine forest and the pretty Lochan Deò.

Take your lunch and sit by the Lily Loch with the mountains in the distance, or wander through the woods in the evening. Midge repellent is recommended — as with any lochside excursion.

A peaceful walk around the far shores of Loch an Eilein, taking in fine woodland, mountain and lochside scenery without steep gradients.

The highlight of this short walk through woodland to lochs Garten and Mallachie is to see ospreys, but there are also rewards in the gentle gradients, beautiful scenery and great variety of birdlife.

Loch Muick was greatly loved by Queen Victoria, who often visited the waterfall at Glas Allt and picnicked on the sandy beach at the head of the loch.

This is a long but satisfying walk to the summit of Lochnagar and the Falls of the Glas Allt, taking in a circuit of Loch Muick.

The initial climb of 1,600ft (490m) to the summit of Morrone gives staggering views of Deeside, Lochnagar and other Cairngorm summits. The bare moorland supports good flocks of grouse and mountain hares.

This walk should be attempted only in the summer months and will require an early start. The route is long and arduous but is rewarded with stunning views of the Cairngorm plateau.

Introduction to the Cairngorms

The majority of people get their first view of the Cairngorms as they drive northwards up the A9 from Perth. At first the mountains lie low on the horizon, their great bulk disguised by distance. Later they grow to dominate the view ahead and serious walkers and climbers will feel elation as they view the dark corries rising gloriously and precipitously to craggy summits. The range covers about 300 sq miles (777 sq km) which make the Cairngorms the most extensive mountainous area to be found in Britain. Geologically it belongs to the Grampian mountain system, the massif which lies at the heart of the Scottish Highlands. The River Dee flows from the eastern side of the Cairngorms and separates Lochnagar from the other main summits. An important route through the Cairngorms, the Lairig Ghru, follows the Dee upstream to its source and then crosses the

Footpath repairs on the way to Fiacaill

watershed below Ben Macdui to descend to Speyside. The road from Ballater to Grantown-on-Spey via Tomintoul provides a further boundary with Glenlivet (a district famous for its malt whiskies) and the Ladder Hills to the north east.

The A9 from Perth to Inverness follows the course of the River Spey and separates the Cairngorms from more mountains to the west, the Monadhliaths. These are comparatively unspectacular heights, a succession of hills which rarely boast summit crags or easy access routes and are thus usually ignored by walkers. In contrast the Cairngorms rise imperiously to the east of the Spey, their tops often snow-covered and veiled by mist. This beauty has beguiled many walkers and climbers over the years into disregarding the dangers and some have suffered accordingly. The Cairngorms should never be taken lightly so take heed of the warnings which follow.

Words of Caution
This book includes routes which could pose problems to those unaccustomed to walking in high and lonely places. On the high Cairngorm plateau the weather can pose severe problems. A bright and sunny day at lower levels can become less agreeable after you have climbed a thousand or so feet (300m). While people sunbathe on Loch

Morlich's beaches it can be blowing a blizzard on the mountain plateau less than four miles (6.5km) away. Mist is potentially a killer once you become lost and some paths are difficult to see even in perfect conditions. In springtime and early summer deep snow lingers in many places and is particularly dangerous when it covers rough ground. Rotten snow gives way without warning and even a short fall can break a leg or an ankle.

Fresh snow causes more obvious problems, especially if it is driven by a gale-force wind so that it is hardly possible to see further than an outstretched hand. At such times it is essential to know exactly where you are and which direction to take to reach safety. *Never go to the Cairngorm tops without adequate warm, waterproof clothing, maps, compass, whistle, emergency rations and a first-aid kit.* Practise using map and compass in good conditions at a place where you know the landmarks and be sure to hear a weather forecast before deciding to tackle any route taking you higher than about 2500 ft (760m). *It is also sensible to tell family and friends where you plan to walk each day.* The Met Office weather forecast for the East Highlands can be checked on their website www.metoffice.gov.uk

Moss campion — a flower of the tundra

Vegetation and Geology

The Cairngorm vegetation reflects the varied climates encountered as you climb higher at this latitude. The river valleys are comparatively verdant and well wooded. Loch Morlich, at about 1000 ft (300m) above sea level, is surrounded by pine trees and has sandy beaches where people lie and sunbathe in the summer. The characteristic vegetation of the ancient Caledonian forest, Scots pines with underlying juniper bushes and blaeberries, is encountered up to a height of about 1600 ft (490m) though at this altitude the junipers will have disappeared and the pines will be very stunted. Rothiemurchus means 'the plain of the great pine', and the forest is one of the last areas of naturally regenerating pine forest in Britain. It may also claim to be the most beautiful, with birches mingling with the Scots pines at low levels making the forest particularly beautiful in the autumn, especially where it fringes the lochs.

Heather will easily survive this high but becomes sparse above 2500 ft (760m) by which time the characteristic sub-arctic tundra vegetation of the plateau will have taken over with mat grass, three-leaved and sedge rush as well as dwarf willow and various mosses. There is also reindeer moss (*Cladonia rangiferina*) which helps to support the herd of reindeer introduced into the Cairngorms 45 years ago, and examples of Alpine flora like starry saxifrage and moss campion whose flowers are such a surprise on the bare, pink granite. This rose-coloured rock is the main bedrock of the highland area. One of the most ancient rocks to be found in Britain, it burst from the core of the earth like a molten fist and solidified as it cooled. The great heat produced in this plutonic episode altered surrounding rock and also created 'cairngorms', beautiful smoky gemstones with colours ranging from yellow through red to black. Later geological activity, about 500 million years ago, distorted the granitic intrusion and the surrounding strata, but the granite remained at the core of the system through the millennia, gradually being reduced by the elements. In recent geological time, during the Ice Age, glaciers gouged out great corries at the start of their course from the tops of the mountains, flowed down to chisel distinctive U-shaped valleys, and ended by dumping debris to form morraines, glacial lakes and so on as they melted.

The summit of Cairn Gorm

Wildlife

The variety of countryside found in the district provides an equally wide range of habitats for wildlife. The native pine forest supports small uncommon birds like crested tits, redwings and crossbills, with siskins comparatively common. This is one of the final retreats of the native red squirrel and these delightful animals appear to be shy of humans but not of dogs. They delight in swearing at dogs from the safety of a tree when they have been disturbed in their foraging. Deer only roam in the lower parts of the forest in midwinter when food is scarce elsewhere.

Of the birds of prey, the osprey steals the limelight from the golden eagle in the Cairngorms. The RSPB's breeding site on Loch Garten is nationally famous and in summer the ospreys overfly a considerable tract of country in search of food. Equally attractive is the peregrine falcon which has a well-known breeding site amongst the crags of Craigellachie overlooking Aviemore. In many other parts of Britain the peregrine has suffered from pesticide poisoning but it appears to escape this in north east Scotland.

The mountain tops provide an environment akin to that of the arctic so it is hardly surprising that the species of northern latitudes should flourish. The snow bunting nests amongst the boulders on the plateau while the dotterel prefers smoother ground. The ptarmigan is probably the best known of all the mountain birds of the Cairngorms though you will be very fortunate to see one even though, like the dotterel, it nests on bare rock.

Lower down the mountain, where the vegetation is more abundant, game birds like red and black grouse and, much more rarely, capercaille will be found. Stocks of the latter are very depleted, probably because it is a large bird which doesn't fly very well – it has been described as a flying turkey. Mountain hares are particularly abundant on moorland to the west of the Spey but may be encountered almost anywhere. They run beautifully, sometimes pausing and standing on back legs to look for signs of pursuit. Their blue-grey coats turn white in winter.

Footnotes

This brings us to points which affect walkers in the area today. Long 'walk-ins' to the mountains are a characteristic of the Cairngorms. Many of the most famous routes are long linear excursions which use mountain passes to cross the watershed from Speyside to Deeside. Road access to the passes is restricted so that often it takes two or three hours' walking before the landscape becomes notably mountainous. The low level walks can be tackled at any time of year, but the higher you go the more circumspect you should be. None of the longer, higher routes should be undertaken until early summer. The Lairig Ghru keeps its snowfields into June, and since they cover streams and boulder fields this is one of the routes best left until the snow has completely melted. There is a magical short time when you can walk almost anywhere on the plateau without treading on snow yet still see it clinging to north-facing corries and crevices. July, still with long days, is a good time for walking even though the infernal midge begins to become active near most lochs. August sees the beginning of the grouse season which brings restrictions on access to some areas and this continues until December, though the most important shoots take place at the beginning of this period.

Goldfinches love the pine forests

Deer stalking takes place between mid-August and mid-October when red deer stags are in prime condition. If a cull did not take place the over-population of deer would lead to great suffering by the animals and harm to farmland as they desperately tried to find food in winter. Stalking brings some restrictions to walkers who will obviously not want to get in the way of a high velocity bullet. Take heed of notices and if possible telephone the estate you will be walking over to make sure that the date is clear. Where possible, relevant telephone numbers are given in the text for the walks while tourist information offices usually have up-to-date details of restrictions. A selection of useful numbers is listed on p.93-95.

Loch Garten and Loch Mallachie

Start	2 miles east of Boat of Garten	
Distance	1¾ miles (2.75km)	
Height gain	Negligible	
Approximate time	1 hour	
Parking	RSPB car park for woodland walks (not the one for the ospreys)	
Ordnance Survey maps	Landranger 36 (Grantown & Aviemore), Explorer OL57 (Cairn Gorm & Aviemore)	

GPS waypoints

- NH 971 185
- Ⓐ NH 969 182
- Ⓑ NH 965 174

This is a very short walk into the RSPB's reserve at Loch Garten famous for its nesting ospreys (though the hide for observing the nest site is about ½ mile to the east and is reached from a different car park). There is always the possibility of seeing one of the ospreys flying to or from the nest while on this walk which takes you to the shores of a pair of beautiful lochs, with views of the long ridge of the Kincardine Hills beyond.

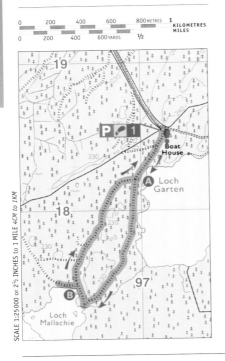

From the RSPB car park take the woodland trail southwards through the forest. This is part of Abernethy Forest, the largest area of native pinewoods in Scotland. The RSPB reserve now covers over 31,000 acres (12,545 ha) and is renowned for its ospreys – birds of prey living primarily from fishing – which have bred here since 1959.

Many of the other species of birds to be seen in the reserve may lack the glamour and publicity value of the ospreys but are still of great interest to ornithologists.

When the trail forks in about 150yds go left. When it forks again, keep right then go left at a third fork Ⓐ. From this path you catch occasional glimpses of Loch Garten through the trees on the left and it is well worth diverting to the loch

Loch Mallachie

shore. The loch is fringed by pine trees and heather, and the western summit of the Kincardine Hills, Craiggowrie, draws the eye to the south. In the autumn and winter wildfowl come to roost here at night, including large flocks of greylag geese and goosanders.

The path leaves Loch Garten and goes through a short section of forest before coming to Loch Mallachie which is even more beautiful with exceptionally straight, tall pine trees. There is a beautiful island with eight trees just offshore and many delightful spots to linger. Take time to divert left at a path junction **B** to wander a little farther round the shore. You may come across some of the specially provided nestboxes around the edge of the two lochs. They are used by Goldeneyes. The male is distinctive in black and white plumage with a white spot below each eye. The female lacks this spot and has a brown head. Goldeneyes rarely nest in Britain and it is estimated that a quarter of the British population is to be found on this reserve.

Retrace your steps to **B** and turn left to follow the trail markers bearing green/blue blazes through the forest. Woodland birds to look out for here include crested tits, siskins and Scottish crossbills. The forest also supports red squirrels. In about ten minutes you reach the outward part of the route and in another five you will be back at the car park. ●

Glen Banchor and Craggan from Newtonmore

		GPS waypoints	
Start	Glen Road, Newtonmore	📝 NN 715 991	
Distance	3 miles (4.75km)	Ⓐ NN 714 998	
Height gain	345 feet (105m)	Ⓑ NN 712 997	
Approximate time	1½ hours	Ⓒ NN 712 996	
Parking	Car parks on Glen Road before church. The one nearest the church is reserved for churchgoers on Sundays	Ⓓ NN 708 993	
		Ⓔ NN 703 997	
Ordnance Survey maps	Landranger 35 (Kingussie & Monadhliath Mountains) and Explorer OL56 (Badenoch & Upper Strathspey)		

This short walk, which makes a delightful evening stroll, wanders through pastures and woodland to Craggan, a fine viewpoint above the upper reaches of the Spey valley. The return follows the river, and on hot evenings the air will resound to the shrieks and screams of children bathing in the refreshing waters of the infant Spey as it twists through a wooded gorge at the start of its long journey to the North Sea.

📝 Glen Road begins from Newtonmore's main street opposite the war memorial and village hall. Walk past the church and follow the road as it bends left then head steadily uphill. Turn right onto a lane opposite a house called Neadaich and follow this uphill. Continue past a cottage to reach a gate. Go through this and follow a grassy track diagonally right across a field, through another gate and on towards a couple of ancient pine trees. Veer left at the trees and keep going to intersect a track. Turn left onto this and continue to reach a junction by a fingerpost Ⓐ. Turn left on to an ancient grooved track that curves around the flank of the hill through a birch wood.

The track passes a cairn then goes through a kissing-gate. Shortly after this at a track junction a fingerpost points to Craggan Ⓑ. Turn left and head uphill on a faint footpath through the trees to reach the viewpoint Ⓒ where a well-situated seat offers the chance for a rest. This lovely spot gives views over the village and the Spey valley to the Cairngorms to the east.

Newtonmore grew up because of its strategic position on General Wade's military road which crossed the Corrieyairack Pass to reach Inverness. It grew in size after tenants in Glen Banchor were moved from their crofts to the village to make way for sheep. The poverty which was in evidence at that time lead to its being described by Queen Victoria as 'a very long poor village'.

Today its situation by the main

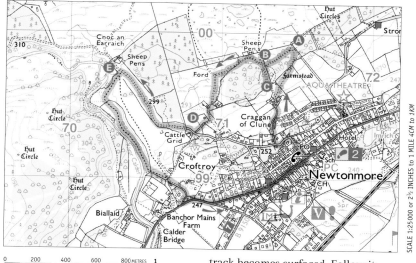

SCALE 1:25 000 or 2½ INCHES to 1 MILE 4CM to 1KM

```
0    200   400   600   800 METRES   1
                                      KILOMETRES
                                      MILES
0    200   400   600 YARDS   ½
```

railway line and trunk road makes it important as a tourist centre. The Clan Macpherson museum at Newtonmore has many mementoes of the clan's ardent support for the Stewart cause during the campaigns of 1715 and 1745. The Chief was a fugitive in these parts for eight years after Culloden, using hideouts close to the then newly built Cluny Castle, the clan head-quarters, before managing to escape to France. The castle was torched by government supporters but was rebuilt and was one of the Highland properties which Queen Victoria considered before she settled at Balmoral. Unhappily the Macphersons left it more than 50 years ago. The annual gathering of the Clan Macpherson takes place at Newtonmore and Kingussie over the first weekend in August.

From the viewpoint retrace your steps to Ⓑ and bear left, rejoining the track. This keeps to the periphery of birch woodland with views across open moorland to the right. Pass several Wildcat Trail markers and go through a couple of pairs of pedestrian gates. At the properties of Golden Acre and Upper Knock the track becomes surfaced. Follow it downhill to meet Glen Road by a cattle-grid Ⓓ. Turn right following a sign pointing to Glen Banchor.

A short stretch of road follows over open moorland and this gradually descends to a fingerpost and track junction on the left Ⓔ. Turn left off the road on to a path which follows the eastern side of the beautiful wooded glen. The River Calder flows through a gorge with waterfalls and deep pools, the latter making good bathing places in hot weather. Eventually the path reaches a burial ground and then goes through a kissing-gate to join a lane. A famous sign, written in Gaelic, points to the burial ground. In English it means 'The road established by law to St Bride's graveyard' and it was put up in 1876 after a farmer had attempted to build over the path. The graveyard takes its name from an anchorite's cell situated here dedicated to Brigid of Kildare who lived in the 6th century and was canonised as St Bride. Robert Louis Stevenson is supposed to have been inspired to write *Catriona* while contemplating a gravestone here.

When the lane from the burial ground meets the main road turn left to return to Newtonmore. ●

Craigendarroch

		GPS waypoints
Start	Craigendarroch Walk, Ballater	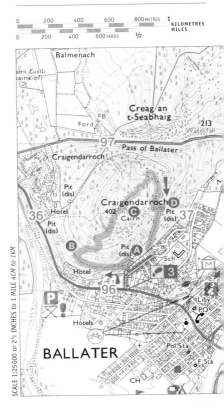 NO 365 960
Distance	1½ miles (2.4km)	**A** NO 365 961
Height gain	640 feet (195m)	**B** NO 362 963
Approximate time	1½ hours	**C** NO 365 965
Parking	On road at start	**D** NO 368 965
Ordnance Survey maps	Landranger 44 (Ballater & Glen Clova), Explorer OL59 (Aboyne, Alford & Strathdon)	

Craigendarroch ('the rocky hill of the oak wood') is the steep granite hill dominating Ballater from the north. Although only just over 1,300ft (400m) high it is nevertheless one of Deeside's finest viewpoints. The crag is best climbed early or late in the day, when Lochnagar's crags and corries are lit by low light which also warms the foliage of the trees on the hills and along the riverbanks.

Craigendarroch Walk is the name given to a housing development on the western side of Ballater, situated about ¼ mile from the town centre on the A93.

There is a waymarked walk starting from here. It's clearly marked at the beginning of the road and there are no problems parking nearby on the straight stretch of road. Go through a kissing-gate and follow a clearly defined path uphill. This climbs behind the houses through mature woods of oak, birch and pine. When you reach a junction marked by a red waymarker **A** turn left.

The path now circles up and round the side of the hill. When you come to a seat look at a retractable interpretation fingerpost that tells how these woods were once coppiced to provide wood for cartwheels. When horse drawn transport ended, so too did the need to keep coppicing the woods but if you look carefully you will still see a few trees with

The view from Craigendarroch

multiple stems.

When you come to the next red waymarker **B** turn right and head uphill. The path gets steadily steeper and rockier. It's a fairly strenuous climb to the top so take your time and move slowly with small steps. If you feel you are getting out of breath then you are going too fast so slow down.

Eventually you will reach the summit where a large cairn **C** over-looks Ballater and the caravan site below. This is not the best of views but in all other directions the views are superb. On a clear day you can see the peak of Lochnagar to the south-west.

Go past the cairn towards a smaller one with a viewfinder. Go past this to pick up the red waymarked downward path and keep on that. *Take care on the descent as it is rather steep.* At a waymark by a bench **D** turn right. After passing another bench you will reach a T-junction, here turn right following a red waymarker arrow. Look out for another interpretation fingerpost this time about insect hotels. Oaks are the best trees in Britain for insects and the trees here often grow a second set of leaves in summer. In times of famine acorns from these trees were ground down to produce flour used in bread making. Acorn flour is very bitter and would only have been used when there was nothing else available.

From here keep on downhill to go through a small gate then along a fenced area to reach the road. Cross this to a red waymarker, then turn right and follow the road back to the start of the walk.

Boat of Garten

		GPS waypoints
Start	Boat of Garten Community Hall	

		GPS waypoints
Start	Boat of Garten Community Hall	🖊 NH 936 189
Distance	4 miles (6.2km)	Ⓐ NH 932 190
Height gain	160 feet (50m)	Ⓑ NH 930 181
Approximate time	2 hours	Ⓒ NH 938 177
Parking	Community Hall car park, signposted down Craigie Avenue from Deshar Road, the main road through the village	Ⓓ NH 945 191
Ordnance Survey maps	Landranger 36 (Grantown & Aviemore), Explorer OL57 (Cairn Gorm & Aviemore)	

Boat of Garten is a peaceful village with several waymarked paths. This fairly level route combines the Red Squirrel and Salmon Trails to make a circuit of varied wildlife habitats. It starts through a pine wood that is home to red squirrels, deer and a variety of bird life, before returning across farmland bordering the River Spey, where both anglers and ospreys hunt salmon and trout.

Note - new houses are being built at the western edge of the village, not yet shown on the map.

The village grew up around a railway station that was built here in the 1860s and named Boat of Garten after the ferry that served the local area. The line was closed in the Beeching cuts, but reopened in the 1970s as the Strathspey Railway, which uses mainly steam locomotives to run tourist trips. This walk also intersects with the Speyside Way and National Cycle Network route 7.

🖊 Walk back up Craigie Avenue and turn left along Deshar Road. Beyond a bay with recycling bins, veer left onto the signposted walk and cycle path that runs parallel to the road.

At a small car park in the trees Ⓐ turn left, pass a metal gate and follow a wide path straight ahead through an open pinewood. Heather, bilberry, cowberry and moss grow under the straight-stemmed trees.

Look out for a bird and red squirrel feeder at a junction and here turn right down a broad track. It leads into the heart of the wood, where rare capercaillie breed. These ground nesting grouse are easily disturbed, so keep dogs under close control.

Turn left at a wide crossroads Ⓑ onto a path signposted Kinchurdy Road. In 500 yards leave the Red Squirrel Trail where it turns left towards Creag Bheag and keep straight ahead to a metal barrier. Go through the gate beside it, cross over the tarmac of Kinchurdy Road and take the path ahead, signposted Dalvoult via Salmon Trail. With care cross over the Strathspey Railway. Now the path runs downhill through a delightful birch wood with clumps of juniper and large, old pines.

Where the path meets a track Ⓒ turn left into more open ground,

Upstream view along the Spey from Garten Bridge

where sheep and cattle may be grazing. The track soon bends left and runs below a wooded slope with riverside fields on the right. Beyond a gate and a white cottage at Dalvoult, the track surface becomes gravelly. Continue for about a mile, passing fishing bothies. Eventually the track rises up the slope to give a view of the golf course on the left. Go over a cattle grid, past bungalows and join the road by tennis courts **D**.

Head right about 100 yards onto Garten Bridge to enjoy the view up the Spey to the mountains. Then return past the tennis courts and turn left into the centre of the village. The road bends right again beside the **Boat Hotel**, The Strathspey Railway station and an attractive little community garden. Continue along the road, passing Victorian villas, shops, café and restaurant. At Craigie Avenue turn left to return to the Community Hall. ●

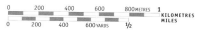

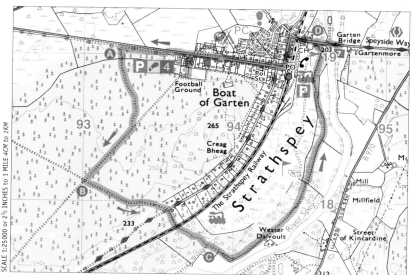

The Braes of Abernethy from Dorback Lodge

		GPS waypoints	
Start	At the end of the public road from Nethy Bridge	🖉	NJ 077 168
Distance	4¼ miles (6.8km)	Ⓐ	NJ 081 169
		Ⓑ	NJ 094 152
Height gain	460 feet (140m)	Ⓒ	NJ 093 152
Approximate time	2½ hours	Ⓓ	NJ 088 147
Parking	Considerate laneside parking before the end of the road		
Ordnance Survey maps	Landranger 36 (Grantown & Aviemore), Explorer OL58 (Braemar, Tomintoul, Glen Avon)		

Dorback Lodge is important as a centre where several long-distance hill tracks reach the civilisation of a metalled highway. However, it is unlikely that you will meet with anyone if you try this route which, on its outward leg, follows the northern side of the Dorback Burn into the romantic Braes of Abernethy. A little easy trail blazing is called for about two miles along this track when you leave it to follow the Allt nan Gamhuinn to reach the track on the other side of the valley. This gives glorious views northwards as it leads past a deserted farm to a ford over the Dorback Burn which might be difficult to cross after prolonged wet weather. It would be wise to check this first.

Note that the Braes of Abernethy should not be confused with the historic village in Perthshire or the famous Abernethy biscuit invented by a surgeon, John Abernethy (1764–1831). A 'brae' is a steep slope overlooking a river or burn. Here the Braes are the upper part of Abernethy Forest, the largest area of natural pine forest surviving in Britain.

🖉 Walk past the boarded-up lodge and the kennels, and then fork right Ⓐ after the latter. Keep ahead when another track leaves to the right just before the second gate after the kennels. The track closely follows the course of the burn at first and can be

seen climbing the hillside for miles ahead. Keep ahead again when another track leaves to the left heading up the slopes of Tom na Fianaig. The track eventually comes to a ford Ⓑ.

Instead of fording the burn here follow it down to reach the Dorback Burn by a solitary pine tree. Cross over the main stream Ⓒ and then follow the Allt na h-Eirghe upstream (south westwards). This part of the walk will be slow going, especially at times when the stream is flowing strongly and you are forced on to the heathery slopes above. If the water level is low progress will be easier and the stream will be crossed a

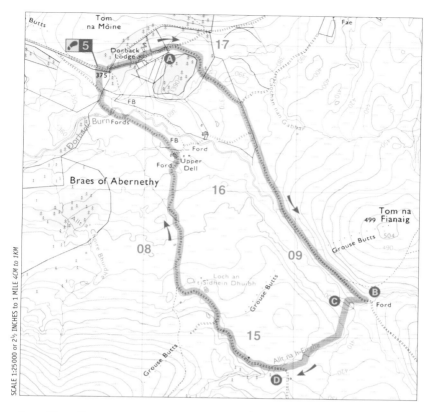

SCALE 1:25000 or 2½ INCHES to 1 MILE 4CM to 1KM

```
0    200   400   600   800 METRES  1
                                    KILOMETRES
                                    MILES
0    200   400   600 YARDS    ½
```

number of times. You will probably be on the south side of the Allt na h-Eirghe when a group of pine trees comes into view. At this point **D** the burn is forded by another track. Turn right on to this.

The track gives wonderful views over a famous tract of countryside, the Braes of Abernethy, as it winds its way back to Dorback. The braes are unusual in having generated sand dunes which rise above the banks of the river. These were initially caused by glacial deposits, later helped by the efforts of a thriving rabbit population. When the track reaches Upper Dell pass it then turn left. Head downhill onto a faint trail that follows a line of telegraph poles across rough

grazing to reach a ford. Cross here, go through a gate and head uphill on a sandy track. Go through a gate in the deer fence, turn right and follow the fence uphill to go through another gate at the start. ●

In the Braes of Abernethy

The Lily Loch and Loch an Eilein from Inverdruie

Start	Inverdruie
Distance	6 miles (9.7km)
Height gain	445 feet (135m)
Approximate time	3 hours
Parking	Public car park at Inverdruie
Ordnance Survey maps	Landranger 36 (Grantown & Aviemore), Explorer OL57 (Cairn Gorm & Aviemore)

GPS waypoints

- 🖉 NH 901 110
- Ⓐ NH 904 099
- Ⓑ NH 900 095
- Ⓒ NH 897 085
- Ⓓ NH 905 077
- Ⓔ NH 917 086

Lochan Mor is better known to locals than to visitors as one of the scenic gems of the Cairngorms. Locals call it the Lily Loch and, fringed by pine trees and with its abundance of water lilies, it makes an enchanting picture in the summer. The walk makes a pleasant evening stroll (though you may need anti-midge precautions) and is an undemanding six-mile circuit with no taxing gradients. If you arrive at Loch an Eilein in the late afternoon you will see exhausted walkers who have completed the 20 miles of the Lairig Ghru from Deeside.

Long before the invention of Aviemore as a resort, Inverdruie was important as a centre of the timber industry. Pine trees from the Rothiemurchus Forest were brought to the village to be sawn into planks. Each spring the timber was heaped on to rafts made of logs and launched into the Spey to float down to the mouth of the river guided by two men, both wielding oars to manoeuvre the raft and prevent it from going aground.

🖉 Turn left out of the car park onto the road then, in a short distance turn left through a gap in the fence onto the mountain bike road to Loch an Eilein, then left onto another road. Turn right on to a path which winds through the woods. The path emerges from the trees and joins a broad well-surfaced cycle path. *Watch out for cyclists.* When a narrow path forks off to the left Ⓐ the cyclists depart on that. Keep straight ahead. This is a lovely part of the route through the ancient pines of the Rothiemurchus Forest.

Rothiemurchus means 'the grand plain of the fir trees' and it has been in the Grant family since 1574. The seat of this sept of the clan is at the Doune, the mansion about one mile south-west of Inverdruie. Fittingly the emblem of Clan Grant is a sprig of Scots pine.

The Lily Loch, officially the Lochan Mor, comes into view suddenly Ⓑ. First there is an enticing glimpse of brilliant blue water through the trees and then a little farther on the lilies appear in all their glory (providing that you are actually here in the right season). It is an idyllic spot to linger on a hot day with the mountains blue in the distance.

Bear right and walk along the northern shore of the loch, passing a cottage to the right before coming to a road by Milton Cottage. Turn left and walk down the quiet road, but fork left **C** at the entrance to the Loch an Eilein car park and turn left onto the public footpath to Braemar by the Lairig Ghru. Continue along the lochside for just over ¹/₂ mile to cross a bridge at a junction of tracks **D**. Follow the one signposted for Laraig Ghru – Glen Eanaich. At a fork in the road turn left following the cyclists sign. Go through the next crossing of paths to reach another crossroads where you turn left following the signposts to Coylumbridge. Keep on this track to go through a gate in a deer fence. Go through a gate and in a couple of hundred feet turn left **E** over a small footbridge, then make your way uphill to reach the public road beside Whitewell. Go north along the road, crossing a cattle-grid and passing Upper Tullochgrue, where Lord Gordon found refuge for a time after the 1745 Jacobite uprising. At Blackpark another road joins from the left. Bear right and continue to follow the road back to Inverdruie. You will meet very little traffic on the way. ●

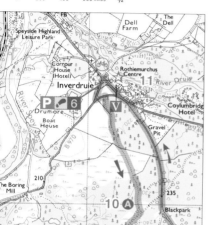

Creag Bheag and Loch Gynack from Kingussie

Creag Bheag and Loch Gynack from Kingussie

Start	Kingussie
Distance	4¼ miles (6.7km)
Height gain	835 feet (255m)
Approximate time	2½ hours
Parking	Kingussie central car park
Ordnance Survey maps	Landranger 35 (Kingussie & Monadhliath Mountains), Explorer OL56 (Badenoch & Upper Strathspey)

GPS waypoints

- 🗺 NH 755 007
- Ⓐ NH 753 008
- Ⓑ NH 748 009
- Ⓒ NH 745 015
- Ⓓ NH 738 017
- Ⓔ NH 752 023

This walk, in the south-west of the area where the River Spey separates the Cairngorms from the less spectacular Monadhliath range, takes you to the top of Creag Bheag, a fine rocky hill to the north of the village which provides wonderful views of the Cairngorm summits over the Spey valley. There are also views to the north beyond beautiful Loch Gynack, tree-fringed on its southern shore. Note: the climb up to Creag Bheag is steep and rocky

Kingussie, 'the head of the pinewood', was founded in the late 18th century by the Duke of Gordon on the opposite side of the Spey to Ruthven, the site of an earlier settlement where the Comyn of Badenoch had a castle and barracks were built by the government after the 1715 Jacobite Rising. In the 1745 Jacobite Uprising the barracks were successfully defended by Sergeant Molloy and 12 men against a besieging force of 300 Jacobites. The building was abandoned after Culloden and is now a romantic ruin well seen from the A9 trunk road. Like neighbouring Newtonmore, Kingussie has a notable shinty team and the game has been administered from here since 1993.

🗺 From the car park toilets follow the direction for Creag Beagh shown by the finger board. Cross a grassy area then turn right and up some steps to reach West Terrace. Turn right and where the road bends right by the Middle Terrace sign Ⓐ keep ahead on a track fingerposted to Creag Beach. After 100 yds turn left through a metal gate and follow a well-waymarked path uphill through the woods. Pass through the remains of a deer fence and continue to follow the well defined path ignoring any turn offs. Eventually it will bend left to reach another waymarker by a junction. Keep straight ahead here. Just beyond the next waymarker the path becomes steep and stony. Climb up from here and through a gap in the deer fence Ⓑ to reach a fingerpost. Follow the direction arrow on this uphill towards Creag Bheag.

The clear path that rises from here has a wall to the right at first as it climbs through heather to the top of Creag Bheag (1597ft/487m). After the

SCALE 1:27777 or about 2¼ INCHES to 1 MILE 3.6CM to 1KM

| 0 | 200 | 400 | 600 | 800 METRES | 1 | | KILOMETRES |
| 0 | 200 | 400 | 600 YARDS | ½ | | | MILES |

rough heather to join a path at the bottom  **D** leading to the shore of Loch Gynack. This proves to be a delightful part of the walk although there is deep heather and bog in places. At the east end of Loch Gynack pick up the waymarkers for the golf course circular walk and go through a gate into a wooded area.

At the end of this wooded area follow the waymarks skirting the ruined Croft of Toman an Sèomair **E** then continue along a high bank. At a waymarker in a dip turn left, then right at the next marker and follow the path through woodland.

Another waymark indicates a left turn. This is followed by a narrow steep downhill section with a handrail. The path eases as you reach a burn. Continue to reach a foot-bridge over the burn, then keep on the path to reach a T-junction with a tarred lane. A fingerpost here indicates a right turn to head to Kingussie. Follow this down through the beautiful glen. Go past white gates and then, opposite the first house (Tigh Mor) take a path which leads down to another footbridge across the Gynack Burn. This one is built over a gorge where the water flows over cascades and through swirl pools. Turn left on to the road on the other side and follow this down to the car park entrance just before the main road. ●

end of the wall rest occasionally and enjoy the fine views back over Kingussie. The first cairn on the summit ridge **C** proves to be one of a series (there are at least six). Continue north to see the view down to Loch Gynack from what is probably the summit cairn. The peak on the other side of the loch is Creag Dhubh which is also the battle cry of the Clan Macpherson. On the south-west side of the hill is Cluny's Cave which served as a hideout both for the chief of the Clan, Ewen Macpherson, and the fugitive Bonnie Prince Charlie after the defeat at Culloden. Ewen evaded capture for eight years after this before eventually following the Prince to exile in France. After enjoying the view over the loch turn back to walk west, passing a lochan, on a path which later becomes indistinct amid deep heather and bog. Blue hares love these slopes and seem to delight in playing hide-and-seek with walkers.

As the gradient of descent eases and roughly in line with the loch's south-western end, turn right over

Glen Brown and Tom nam Marbh

		GPS waypoints	
Start	White Bridge, on A939 ½ mile east of Bridge of Brown and 3 miles north-west of Tomintoul	🖊 NJ 133 209	
		Ⓐ NJ 139 209	
Distance	4½ miles (7.3km)	Ⓑ NJ 148 201	
		Ⓒ NJ 136 186	
Height gain	785 feet (240m)	Ⓓ NJ 130 193	
Approximate time	2½ hours		
Parking	Layby at White Bridge		
Ordnance Survey maps	Landranger 36 (Grantown & Aviemore), Explorers OL58 (Braemar, Tomintoul, Glen Avon) and OL61 (Grantown-on-Spey & Hills of Cromdale)		

Glenlivet Estate has many excellent waymarked walks and leaflets can be obtained from the information office in Tomintoul. This is a particularly good walk for children who will love looking for the 'little people' of the Clan MacBog.
Note that deer stalking can affect this walk from the end of April to 12 August and the first three weeks in October. Contact the Estate Information Office Tel: 01479 870 070 or e-mail: info@glenlivetestate.co.uk

🖊 Walk up the track on the edge of the plantation. There are power lines to the right while to the left, at the end of the planting, there is a fine view over Strath Avon. Go over the stile on the edge of the plantation and continue along the old sunken road. You are on a short length of the military road which was constructed in Strath Avon in 1754.

Leave this track when it swings to the left Ⓐ and go right on a well waymarked path to go under some power lines before swinging left and heading downhill at a waymarker by a bench. Stop here for a short while just to admire the fantastic views. Follow the path to a small burn (NJ 141 205) but keep a sharp look out

for the dreaded and notorious Clan MacBog. You may see some of these 'little people' under the gorse bush on your right just after crossing the burn. According to legend they derive their income from attacking unwary travellers, beating them up and stealing their credit cards. However with an average height of just 12cm it is difficult to see how this can be. There may be thousands more of them nearby in the heather. A small plaque near here warns of the danger and tells of captive MacBogs that can be purchased in nearby Tomintoul. Continue to follow the path along the flank of the hill.

The path descends to cross a small birch wood and follows its lower edge

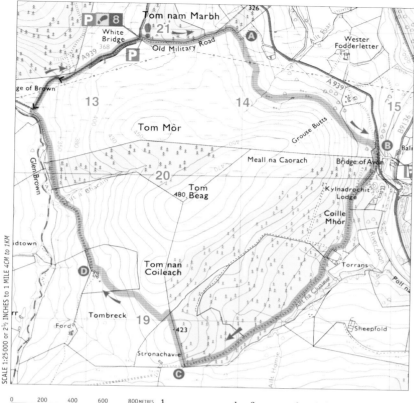

SCALE 1:25 000 or 2½ INCHES to 1 MILE 4CM to 1KM

with a fence to the left. You may well see woodpeckers in the wood. Cross a stile into a pine wood which provides welcome shade on a hot day. The path descends gently to join a forest track **B** near the Bridge of Avon, which is not visible from the walk. On reaching the forest track turn right.

Bear right when the track divides before a cottage and then bear left about 75 yds later. Pass through a gate after about 100 yds. A long steady climb follows through the Kylnadrochit plantation to reach its western edge near Stronachavie, one of many local abandoned farms.

Cross the stile and turn right **C** to follow the edge of the plantation uphill with the ruined farm to the left

and a fence to the right. In early summer there are large multi-coloured violets on the hillside here. After the summit the path drops down to a fence and an old gate. Bear left here away from the forest, enjoying grand views to the left up Glen Brown, and follow another fence for a short way before passing through it at a gateway. The way then drops to reach another ruined croft, Tombreck. One of the crofts in the glen hereabouts flourished for a time, managing to support a family of 14.

Here you join a muddy track **D** and this descends to reach the edge of a plantation just above the Burn of Brown. The track takes you to the main road just above the Bridge of Brown. Turn right and climb up the main road to return to the starting point at White Bridge. ●

GLEN BROWN AND TOM NAM MARBH ● 29

The Five Bridges Walk, Ballater

		GPS waypoints
Start	Ballater	🖊 NO 369 957
Distance	5½ miles (8.7km)	Ⓐ NO 373 955
Height gain	115 feet (35m)	Ⓑ NO 360 949
Approximate time	2½ hours	Ⓒ NO 344 965
Parking	Car park behind Glen Muick church	Ⓓ NO 352 970
Ordnance Survey maps	Landranger 44 (Ballater & Glen Clova), Explorers OL53 (Lochnagar, Glen Muick & Glen Clova) and OL59 (Aboyne, Alford & Strathdon)	

There are no taxing gradients on this low level walk from Ballater which twice crosses the River Dee. The walk runs through Dalliefour Wood where the forest drive provides shade in the summer or shelter if the weather is unkind. The last section of the route, above the River Dee, is especially glorious in autumn.

Ballater cannot claim to be an ancient town since its origins lie in the development of mineral springs at nearby Pananich in the 1790s. However, Queen Victoria's purchase of the Balmoral estate gave real impetus to its growth and the splendid station opposite the town hall was built in memory of Prince Albert. The station saw many regal passengers before its closure as branch lines became uneconomic.

The first of the bridges crossed is the Royal Bridge which spans the Dee on the south-east side of the town. This was opened by Queen Victoria in 1885 to replace a wooden bridge built in 1834. This in turn superseded a stone bridge built by Telford which only lasted for 20 years. All this is testament to the power of the River Dee and to the skill of the designer and builders of the existing bridge.

🖊 Turn right out of the car park on to the main road and walk down to the river. After crossing the bridge turn right Ⓐ and continue along the road by the river.

The second of the bridges to be crossed is the little bridge across the Brackley Burn before the more impressive Bridge of Muick where the road up Glen Muick leaves to the left. The cairn here commemorates an occasion on September 16, 1899 when Queen Victoria attended a presentation of colours to the First Batallion of the Gordon Highlanders just before they embarked for South Africa. Many of the men who marched past her died in the campaign, including their commanding officer, Colonel Dowman. A straight length of road follows, which heads towards the ruin of Knock Castle, a stronghold built in the 16th century by the Huntly Gordons. About ¹⁄₂ mile down this road there is a house called Woodstock on the right and just past it a blue waymarker by the roadside indicates a right turn onto a sandy track.

Take this sandy track **B** into Dalliefour Wood. It provides very pleasant, level walking and you will soon pass Dallyfour Cottage which has a particularly beautiful garden. The track runs straight and true through woodland for one mile or so before reaching the graceful, white painted suspension bridge over the Dee by Polhollick Cottage. Cross the bridge **C**. The building on your right is a gauging station for the River Dee. The cableway running across the river is used to suspend a device that measures the speed of the current. Inside there is a stilling well which provides a flat, wave-free surface and allows permanently installed instruments to continuously measure the water level. Look beside the building and you will see a gauge that lets you see the level at a glance. From here continue along the track to reach the main road (A93).

Cross the road and turn right. After 50 yds there is a gate on the left. Go through this and then turn right on to a path by a blue waymarker. It climbs up above the road and passes through encroaching bushes of broom. They provide an attractive foreground for pictures in the early summer. Follow the path until it descends to go through a gate and cross the

The lovely lochan in the forest

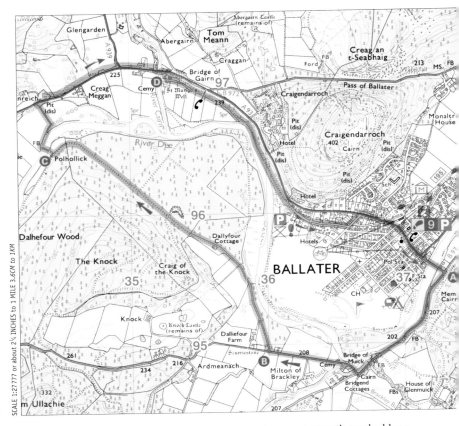

Tomintoul road. Go through another gate and continue on the footpath until it joins the road at Bridge of Gairn **D**.

This is the last of the five bridges and it takes the road over the River Gairn which has its source on the eastern slopes of Beinn a' Bhuird. St Mungo's Well, on the east bank of the Gairn, is dedicated to the memory of the 6th-century saint who founded Glasgow cathedral. He is also known as Kentigern and a church bears his name farther down Deeside at Tulloch. Cross the road and take the path across the bridge. Then turn first right into the driveway of Bridgend of Gairn Farm and then immediately left

onto a narrow path marked by a white waymarker. This footpath gradually drops down to join a track after about 200 yds. This makes a beautiful finale to the walk as it runs through woodland with the river flowing swiftly below. Old milestones by the track testify to its once having been the main road. There is a choice of paths, higher or lower, as you near Ballater; the lower passes through a picnic area before both paths meet again at the end of Old Line Road. When this road reaches the drive to the Balgonie Hotel keep ahead on the path which runs parallel to the Braemar road. However, you will eventually have to turn left into Invercauld Road to reach the main road by the Auld Kirk Hotel where you turn right to reach the town centre. ●

Glen Feshie

		GPS waypoints	
Start	Near Achlean on the east side of Glen Feshie		
		NN 850 985	
Distance	3½ miles (5.5km)	Ⓐ NN 852 971	
Height gain	415 feet (125m)	Ⓑ NN 852 963	
Approximate time	2 hours	Ⓒ NN 850 964	
		Ⓓ NN 852 967	
Parking	Car park 4.5 miles south of Feshiebridge, on single track road signposted 'Lagganlia' and 'Achlean'	Ⓔ NN 859 972	
		Ⓕ NH 854 975	
Ordnance Survey maps	Landranger 35 (Kingussie & Monadhliath Mountains), Explorer OL57 (Cairn Gorm & Aviemore)		

The dynamic River Feshie flows through this wild glen, carving new river banks and depositing fresh gravel banks with every flood. This walk explores the river flats then heads into pine woods to visit an unnamed waterfall on the Allt Fhearnagan, which drops in a splendid series of cascades down pink, water-sculpted granite rocks. The route fords the Allt Fhearnagan twice – it should be fordable in all but severe spates, but crossing dry-shod could prove tricky when the river level is above average.

Glen Feshie is home to many old 'granny' pines as well as younger plantations. New pine and birch trees are springing up in the heather now the estate has reduced the number of grazing sheep and deer.

Go left out of the car park and along the tarmac road to Achlean farm, which remains hidden in a dip until you are almost upon it. Take the footpath to the left of the buildings and fences, following it up a bank onto an area of flat heather moorland. Ignore paths to right and left, keeping ahead past a post. The path curves right then weaves attractively through small humps of moraine.

Go through a gate in a deer fence Ⓐ and immediately ford the Allt Fhearnagan. Continue ahead beside a

pine plantation. Keep left at a fork in the path, staying above the grassy flats to the right, where a bridge can

At the top of the unnamed waterfall

be seen over the River Feshie. Keep on, apparently past the bridge, until a rough vehicle track crosses the path **B**. Turn right along the track to the bridge, where you can enjoy a dramatic view upriver. The grassy river banks here make a good picnic spot **C**.

Return a few paces along the grassy track then fork left onto a narrow gravel path. This runs across flat ground to rejoin the outward path. Turn left and retrace your steps for about 165 yards. Look out on the right for a rough track, marked by a granite kerbstone **D**.

Turn up the track, which is knee deep in heather but shows signs of vehicle use – it is easiest to walk in the ruts where the wheels have cut through the vegetation. Pass to the left of an open area then follow a broad ride through the trees. Keep left where the ride forks and pass above a pool. Look out for the wooden handrail of a footbridge, cross over and keep on in the same direction through shrubby trees to a clearer ride continuing ahead. At the top of the ride, keep left of a stream and emerge into a more open area scattered with grand old pines.

The path bends left then peters out, but by now you are within sight and sound of the waterfall. Head towards it then turn right up a rough path with ever changing views of the cascades. Take care as the path runs close to the drop. At the top, go over

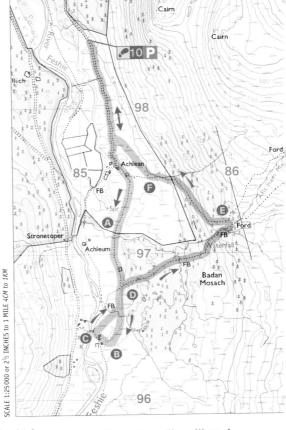

SCALE 1:25 000 or 2½ INCHES to 1 MILE 4CM to 1KM

a lip into a flatter, more open area, leaving the big trees behind. Here ford the Allt Fhearnagan again then head uphill, away from the stream, on pathless ground through trees and heather to gain a good path **E** that runs less than 100 yards above the river.

Turn left down the path, which descends from the Munro Carn Ban Mor above. It soon bends right and views open up to the distant Monadhliath Mountains. Go through a gate and continue down onto flatter ground. Turn right at a fork **F** onto a wide path eroded through the peat. Follow it to rejoin the road north of Achlean and go right, back to the car park. ●

Woodland and riverside from Grantown-on-Spey

		GPS waypoints
Start	Grantown-on-Spey	
Distance	7 miles (11.1km)	NJ 034 280
Height gain	115 feet (35m)	Ⓐ NJ 059 285
Approximate time	3½ hours	Ⓑ NJ 061 286
		Ⓒ NJ 065 289
Parking	Burnfield car park, to the right of Grantown's main street heading north	Ⓓ NJ 055 272
		Ⓔ NJ 053 272
Ordnance Survey maps	Landranger 36 (Grantown & Aviemore), Explorer OL61 (Grantown-on-Spey & Hills of Cromdale)	

This is a walk which divides itself neatly into two: the outward part is through pleasant woodland leading to the River Spey and the homeward half follows the banks of the famous salmon river. This is a reasonably walk and the paths should be dry unless the river is high after prolonged rain.

Turn right from the car park and left at the end of the road. At the next junction turn right into Golf Course Road. When the road bends keep ahead on a path across the golf course and go through a gate into Anagach Wood and onto the Speyside Way, following the yellow waymarkers. Anagach Wood is an important wildfowl breeding site from April 1 to August 15 so keep to the main tracks and keep dogs on a short lead. When the path divides by a seat bear left following the Speyside Way. There is a lovely mixture of trees — tall pines with rowans and birches. At the next junction bear left still on the Speyside Way and with the red waymarkers of a forest walk. Hills can be seen ahead through the trees as the track reaches another junction with a thoughtfully sited seat.

Turn right here still following the red markers and the Speyside Way. The path heads downhill to reach a fence beside a stream with open ground beyond. As the path starts to climb there is a junction on the right where the red path turns off. Keep ahead on the Speyside Way Ⓐ and head uphill into a conifer plantation. After this the way is through a planting of conifers, curving down to another gate and meeting a track

The River Spey near Grantown

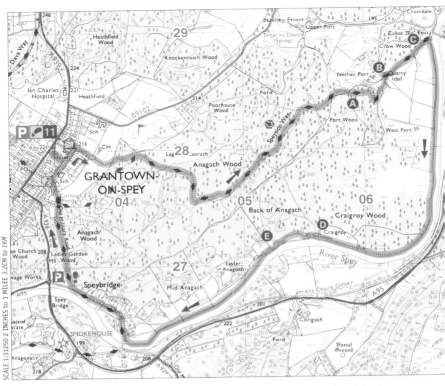

SCALE 1:31250 2 INCHES to 1 MILE 3.2CM to 1KM

| 0 | 200 | 400 | 600 | 800 METRES | 1 |
| 0 | 200 | 400 | 600 YARDS | ½ | |

KILOMETRES
MILES

coming from the right. Bear left here to reach an iron gate, a cattle-grid, and a bridge over a burn. Turn right at a junction **B** to go through a gate and follow a path which meanders beside the river to eventually merge onto a farm track just before Cromdale suspension bridge. Turn right here **C**. The open views and farmland contrast with what has gone before. Herons share the fishing with anglers and there is a vast population of mallard.

After about 20 minutes you will come to a fishermen's hut and enter woodland with the river making a tight curve below. Almost too soon the track comes out of the woodland. There is a pleasant seat to pause at where the track becomes a path rising up the riverbank to Craigroy **D**. Keep to the main track which goes through

scrubby birch wood and juniper. About ¼ mile from Craigroy the electricity line crosses the track which is close to the river. As it swings to the right **E** take a narrow footpath on the left and head downhill through woodland towards the river.

The riverside path passes some of Scotland's best salmon beats and provides excellent walking, often on grass, to reach the Old Bridge at Speybridge. Walk up through the village and after the last house look for a yellow waymarker opposite a small car park. Turn right here, into Anagach Woods and follow the wide drive that is part of General Wade's road into Grantown and now part of the Speyside Way. The golf course is to the right before Wade's road reaches South Street opposite the fire station. Turn right and pass the primary school before taking the first turn left back to Burnfield car park. ●

Creag a Chalamain and Castle Hill

		GPS waypoints
Start	Allt Mor car park	
Distance	8 miles (12.8km)	🖉 NH 983 087
Height gain	1,605 feet (490m)	Ⓐ NH 984 071
Approximate time	4½ hours	Ⓑ NH 974 062
Parking	At start	Ⓒ NH 967 055
Ordnance Survey maps	Landranger 36 (Grantown &	Ⓓ NH 968 064
	Aviemore), Explorer OL57 (Cairn	Ⓔ NH 966 075
	Gorm & Aviemore)	Ⓕ NH 974 083

The approach walk is on excellent paths, either newly constructed or restored and drained. The two hills are pathless, mostly over short heather and stones with thankfully short sections of longer heather at lower levels. The walk passes through beautiful Scots pine woodland, ending on forest roads. The high section is not recommended in mist, though a short cut is detailed below should inclement weather strike.

🖉 From the Allt Mor car park head off in a south-easterly direction indicated by a purple marker post. Almost immediately cross a narrow timber footbridge over the Allt Mor. (The footbridge can be seen from the car park.) After crossing the footbridge turn right, this is the Allt Mor Trail.

Follow the Trail, taking care where it crosses the road, until point Ⓐ is reached. Here another path joins from the road above. Turn right, crossing the Allt Mor on a long footbridge, known as Utsi's Bridge. Take note here of the natural erosion taking place as the Allt Mor carves its way through the glacial deposits, or 'till'. The path zigzags steeply up the far side of the gorge. Just before the top rim of the gorge take a left turn for the path leading to the Chalamain Gap. The Gap comes into view as higher ground is reached. To the left

are superb views into the Northern Corries of the Cairngorm Mountains.

At Ⓑ the burns are easily forded thanks to stepping stones. *Here the narrower right-hand path can be used to cut out the hills in case of inclement weather, going straight to point Ⓓ.* However, assuming conditions permit, keep left and head straight up the steady climb towards the Chalamain Gap. The path is narrower now but still good.

At Ⓒ, as the Chalamain Gap is approached, cross the small burn below the path on the right near a small pool, and before the ground on the right becomes too steep. The start of the climb to Creag a Chalamain is steep and in deep heather but the gradient soon lessens and the heather soon becomes stunted. Keep going straight up and you are bound to reach the rocky summit. The views

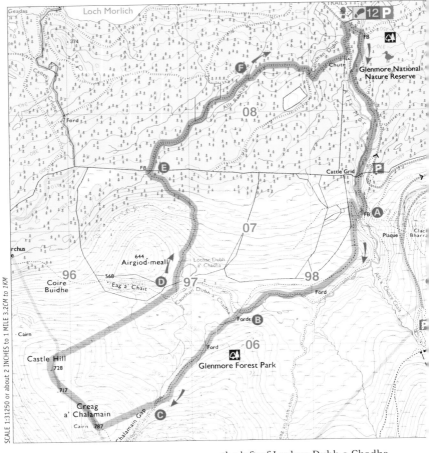

SCALE 1:31250 or about 2 INCHES to 1 MILE 3.2CM to 1KM

```
0    200   400   600   800 METRES 1
                                    KILOMETRES
                                    MILES
0    200   400   600 YARDS   1/2
```

from this, the highest point of the walk, are magnificent, especially those into the Lairig Ghru with Braeriach beyond.

Our route lies north-westwards to the small cairn on Castle Hill. Turn right at this cairn and descend aiming for Lochan Dubh a Chadha. The final section down to the path at the east end of the Eag a Chait (Cat's Gap) is rough going underfoot.

Locate the deer fence at **D** and follow the track east for a few yards until a left turn is seen heading up towards the fence. Reach the fence and follow it for 150 yds to a stile. Cross the stile and follow the path to

the left of Lochan Dubh a Chadha, and over a low col. The path drops down and enters the forest, winding as it does through some beautiful Scots' Pines.

At **E** cross the burn below Utsi's Hut onto the end of a forest road. Follow this to the right to stay next to the burn.

At **F** turn right at the junction of the forest roads. In 500 yds turn left at the next junction of forest roads and follow this to the main road. Just before the junction with the road turn left onto a blue waymarked cycle path. It's a short distance from here to the car park which is concealed in the trees. Look out for the signpost then leave the path to cross the road to the car park. ●

Carrbridge and General Wade's Road

		GPS waypoints
Start	Carrbridge	
Distance	7¾ miles (12.3km)	 NH 907 227
Height gain	625 feet (190m)	Ⓐ NH 896 224
Approximate time	4 hours	Ⓑ NH 895 212
Parking	Carrbridge car park	Ⓒ NH 887 199
Ordnance Survey maps	Landranger 36 (Grantown & Aviemore), Explorer OL57 (Cairn Gorm & Aviemore)	Ⓓ NH 883 199 Ⓔ NH 869 220 Ⓕ NH 891 226 Ⓖ NH 898 230

This is an enjoyable low level ramble through forest and moor and on paths along meadows and riverbanks. The highlight of the walk is General Wade's Road which is followed as far as Sluggan Bridge, a memorable beauty spot. From here a path leads back to Carrbridge, never far from the River Dulnain. Note that after heavy rain there may be difficulty in fording Allt Lorgy.

From the car park on the Aviemore road (B9153) turn right and walk down the road as far as the post office. Turn left here, just before the bridge, on to Station Road. The

The old bridge, Carrbridge

remains of the famous packhorse bridge, built in 1717, can be seen on the right. It was badly damaged in the disastrous flood of August 1829.

Pass the road to the station on the left and go beneath the railway and then the main road (A9). Turn off the

road to the left **A** after passing land awaiting development and immediately before a timber yard. Keep the timber yard to the right and follow the rough road to reach a metal gate at the edge of a wood. Go through the gate and continue along a forest road. When the track forks keep right. Go through a second gate and continue to clear the wooded area. Then look out for a broad green lane **B** just before the track bends left and turn right onto it. Keep following it, go through a wooden gate and continue. The track passes beneath power lines and carries on through a ghostly patch of forest with crimson fungi and trees spangled with lichen. Turn right at a T-junction on to General Wade's Road **C**.

The sandy track leads down to a ford, which is the crossing point of the Allt Lorgy **D**. The crossing itself may call for the removal of boots and socks and the rolling up of trousers. The track climbs and at the top of the hill there is a crossroads. Keep ahead — fine views open up both in front and to the right. The stumps of felled Scots' pines look as though they could well have been standing when General Wade constructed the road during the 18th century. Bear right when a track leaves to the left. After this the road strikes northwards in a straight line and passes beneath power lines. In another 500 yds it crosses a road.

General Wade's Road is now more picturesque as it winds down through pines and birches. It may be very wet at times. At a junction turn left and continue downhill. The highlight of the walk comes as the way opens up and reaches East Sluggan, lush grassland shaded by mature trees. Cross the wonderful packhorse bridge

and then turn right **E** to pass a ruined croft. There is a fine view of the bridge as another path is joined which runs through bracken along the edge of a wood. Climb a high deer gate. On the other side the path is through heather rather than bracken. There are good views of the River Dulnain. The path joins a track of red

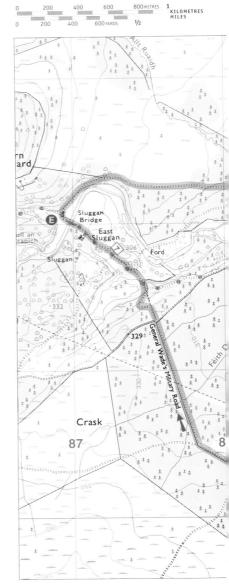

earth which passes a redundant stile and then descends to a deer fence and a burn. After fording the burn the path follows the course of the river closely and the new bridge carrying the A9 is seen ahead. Bear slightly to the left away from the river on to a causeway which takes you to a footbridge 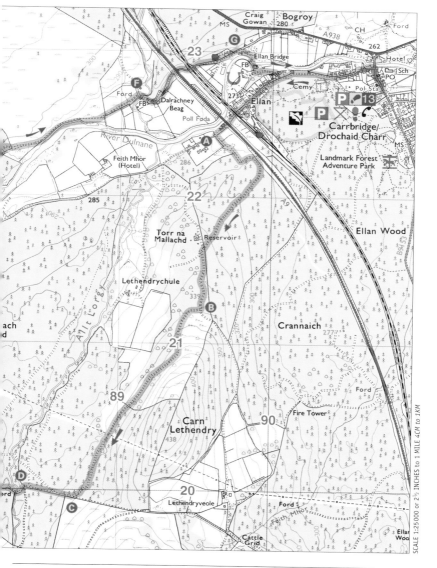 by a house named Lynphail.

After crossing the bridge *(its boards are slippery when wet)* join the track and walk down it to cross the A9 and pass beneath the railway. Continue along the road from the railway bridge, passing some wooden buildings on the right **G**, then turn right on a downhill path leading to a suspension bridge. Over this, turn left when the path meets a track leading to trekking stables. Turn left when the track meets Station Road and follow this back to the main road. Turn right to the car park. ●

SCALE 1:25 000 or 2½ INCHES to 1 MILE 4CM to 1KM

Glen Tilt

		GPS waypoints
Start	Blair Atholl	✏ NN 874 662
Distance	6 miles (9.4km)	Ⓐ NN 876 665
Height gain	150 feet (50m)	Ⓑ NN 877 677
Approximate time	3 hours	Ⓒ NN 877 687
Parking	Glen Tilt car park, reached by crossing the Old Bridge of Tilt then turning left at the first gap in the wall	Ⓓ NN 882 699
		Ⓔ NN 883 682
		Ⓕ NN 882 674
Ordnance Survey maps	Landranger 43 (Braemar & Blair Atholl), Explorers OL49 (Pitlochry & Loch Tummel) and OL51 (Atholl)	

Blair Atholl is the estate village for Blair Castle, the historic home of the Dukes of Atholl, and the centre of vast estates that encompass woods, rivers and mountains. Glen Tilt, a U-shaped glaciated valley, extends north from the village, cutting a deep gap through the Cairngorms, the start of a classic 28-mile hike to Braemar. This walk explores the lower reaches of the glen.

The full Glen Tilt Trail is a 10-mile route waymarked with yellow arrows on posts; this 6-mile walk follows the short cut across Gilbert's Bridge. One of six walks waymarked from Blair Atholl, it has the most dramatic views. Look out for red squirrels and buzzards, or possibly even an eagle or pine marten.

The walk passes through a rifle range. Access is safe when short-range shooting is taking place, providing you keep to the main track. However, a few days a year it is closed during long-range shoots. The timetable is on the car park information board and on the website www.athollestatesrangerservice.co.uk

Glen Tilt woods

 Take a little path to the right of the information board in the car park and in a few paces turn right towards the river. Bear left down to the riverside path. A folly with seats and a balcony lies just to the right, but the route goes left and crosses the

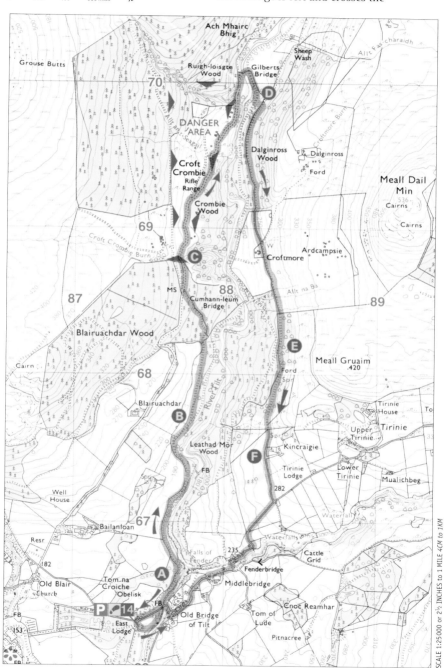

road by an arched stone footbridge. An earth path continues high above the river, then emerges onto the main Glen Tilt track **A**.

Turn right along the track, soon walking with open fields rising on the left. After the track has bent right and gone downhill back into woodland, look for an earth path forking left **B**.

Follow this steadily uphill through a birch wood. Cross over a rushing burn into an open forest of tall Douglas fir and larch. Ignore a grassy way to the right and keep left on the main path, which climbs uphill through the trees. It steepens before reaching an upper track – turn right along this and go through a gateway to the rifle range viewpoint **C**.

The impressive panorama includes the heather-clad Munro Carn a' Chalmain and the grassy hill Meall Dall Min across the glen. Continue over a stone bridge and down the main track through the range, keeping right at three forks along the way. Follow the shortcut waymark across Gilbert's Bridge and turn right on the far side of the River Tilt.

Go over a cattle grid and in 200 yards turn left up a rough path marked by a post in a cairn **D**. This rises steeply through trees to a stile. Go over and turn right along a grassy track with scattered birch trees on the hillside above. Further on, near Croftmore cottage, the view opens up across the glen. The next stretch can be wet and muddy underfoot. Go through a high gate into woodland and keep left at a fork **E**, remaining on the level.

Go through a gate and across a field to another gate below Kincraigie Farm **F**. A tremendous view now stretches ahead over Glen Garry to pyramid-shaped Schiehallion, with white-washed Blair Castle half hidden in the trees below. The view back into the Atholl mountains is equally stunning.

Keep ahead on the farm access track to a tarmac road and turn right down it. It winds down steeply and across Fenderbridge. Keep right to descend to Old Bridge of Tilt and here turn right across the bridge. Continue between walls until the gap on the left leads back to the car park. ●

Looking up Glen Tilt from the rifle range viewpoint

Glen Lui and Derry Lodge

		GPS waypoints
Start	Linn of Dee car park, 6 miles west of Braemar	
Distance	7 miles (11.1km)	
Height gain	330 feet (100m)	
Approximate time	3½ hours	
Parking	At start	
Ordnance Survey maps	Landranger 43 (Braemar & Blair Atholl), Explorers OL57 (Cairn Gorm & Aviemore)	

GPS waypoints

✎ NO 063 898
Ⓐ NO 064 902
Ⓑ NO 063 914
Ⓒ NO 040 933

The track up Glen Lui is the most popular approach to the southern Cairngorms. This walk explores the glen as far as Derry Lodge, an abandoned hunting lodge set in one of the most beautiful corners of the Grampian hills. The route lies on the Mar Lodge Estate, which was acquired by the National Trust for Scotland in 1995. Red deer culling takes place from 1 July to 15 February, and during this period walkers are asked not to deviate from recognised hill tracks, of which this walk is one. A short section of path towards the end of the walk can occasionally be slippery and potentially hazardous, and is not suitable for young children.

✎ From the car park at Linn of Dee take the footpath signposted to Glen Lui. Head uphill on a forest path then downhill and across some duckboards. Eventually reach a Land Rover track and turn left Ⓐ. (There are actually two paths, one from each half of the car park, which converge after about 50 yds. Turn left here, and take note of the East Grampian Deer Management Group information board. One of the aims of the National Trust for Scotland is the regeneration of natural woodland, which involves culling the huge herds of red deer that roam the estate. Many of the Scots pines in Glen Lui are 150 to 200-years-old, but there is very little new growth outside the fenced enclosures because the deer

eat the saplings.

After walking approximately ¾ mile from the gate you cross the Black Bridge over the Lui Water Ⓑ and turn left. From the bridge there is a fine view up the glen towards Derry Cairngorm (the conical summit on the right) and Ben Macdui, which at 4,296ft (1,309m) is the second highest mountain in Britain. The glen here is broad and green, with grassy pastures by the river where herds of red deer are sometimes seen. The valley was once farmed, but the crofters were forcibly evicted in 1726 and, although some people later returned, by 1840 the farms had been completely abandoned. Today all that remains is the occasional ruckle of stones by the roadside marking the ruins of dykes

Mature Scots pines in lower Glen Lui

and cottages.

A further two miles of easy walking brings you to Derry Lodge. Originally built as a hunting lodge for the estate, it was leased in the 1950s to the Cairngorm Club who used it as a base for expeditions into the mountains. It now lies unused, looking rather forlorn with its boarded-up windows. Just past the lodge is a wooden shed containing mountain rescue equipment and an emergency public telephone.

On a sunny day, the edge of the woods at the confluence of the Derry and Luibeg burns makes a fine picnic spot **G**. Here you can recline on a lush bed of grass beside the stream and admire the view towards Luibeg Cottage. Glen Luibeg is the gateway to the Lairig Ghru, probably the finest mountain pass in Britain, leading to Rothiemurchus and Aviemore. Off to your right (north) is Glen Derry, the start of another cross-country walking route over the Lairig an Laoigh to the Fords of Avon, and

then by Bynack More or Strath Nethy to Loch Morlich, or down Glen Avon to Tomintoul.

Begin the return leg of the walk by following the path along the left bank of the Lui Water, which passes the recently rebuilt Bob Scott's Bothy, before rejoining the Land Rover track. (The bothy, destroyed by fire in 2003 was reopened in 2005. What started as a small group 'The Friends of Bob Scott's Association' grew in size as wellwishers and volunteers heard of the plans and pitched in. Funds were raised, plans made and the National Trust for Scotland were persuaded of the wisdom of restoring the bothy.) This and the original bothy commemorated the Mar Lodge gamekeeper who lived in nearby Luibeg cottage in the 1950s and was a great friend to the Hill Stravaigers who frequented these Glens. It's a great place to stop for a break on a wet and windy day or to overnight before taking the classic Lairig Ghru walk.

Retrace the outward route to Ⓐ, then continue along the track down the glen to reach the road. Turn right onto it and follow it back to the car park. ●

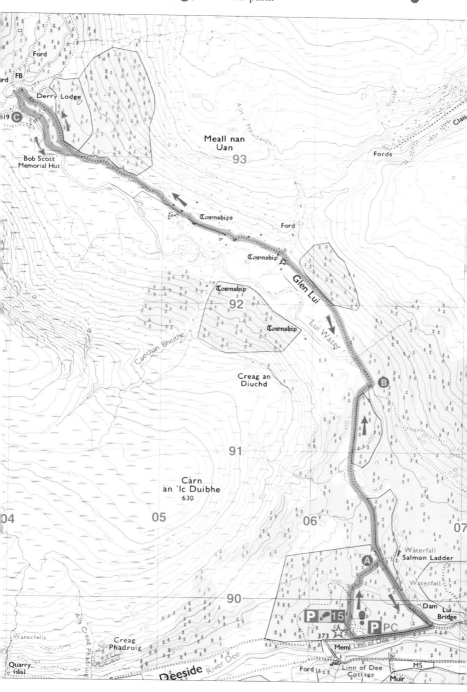

Carn Daimh from Glenlivet (sidebar)

Carn Daimh from Glenlivet

Start	Tomnavoulin
Distance	6½ miles (10.5km)
Height gain	1,150 feet (350m)
Approximate time	3½ hours
Parking	Clash Wood car park. This is reached via the byway which leaves the main road (B9008) to the left as you drive northwards out of the village
Ordnance Survey maps	Landranger 36 (Grantown & Aviemore), Explorer OL61 (Grantown-on-Spey & Hills of Cromdale)

GPS waypoints

- NJ 208 265
- Ⓐ NJ 204 261
- Ⓑ NJ 193 248
- Ⓒ NJ 190 235
- Ⓓ NJ 181 249
- Ⓔ NJ 181 262
- Ⓕ NJ 187 262

This is another of the excellent walks maintained and waymarked by the Glenlivet Estate. It takes you through remote farmland and forest before joining the Speyside Way and then climbing to the summit of Carn Daimh which, at 1,869ft (570m), is a splendid viewpoint. However, the best moment in the walk comes as a finale, when the path drops into Glenlivet and you are faced with a wonderful scene of high, heather covered hills on the far side of the verdant glen.

Walk up the forest track from the car park for about 200 yds before leaving it to the left to follow a 'Walk 5' waymark ('Walk 9' continues ahead). The footpath leaves the forest and skirts pastures with woodland to the right. Go over a stile at the end of the plantation and then cross another stile Ⓐ on to the farm track which leads to Westertown.

Immediately after this point another track, to Easter Corrie, leaves to the right. Ignore this and keep on the lower track to Westertown, perhaps pausing occasionally to enjoy the fine view back to Glenlivet.

After Westertown cross the Allt a' Choire by a plank bridge beside the ford. After passing through a belt of trees the track crosses the Slough Burn (a tributary of Allt a' Choire)

and then climbs steeply to swing left towards Craighead, an abandoned farm. The track stops here to the right of the ruin at two metal gates. Cross a stile Ⓑ at a waymark and keep straight ahead on a grassy footpath heading towards woodland. Cross another two stiles then continue along a narrow footpath crossing open countryside. A steady climb will take you to a gate into the wood. Looking back from here you can see the conical outline of Ben Rinnes (2,755ft/840m) to the north. Downhill to your right by a lone Scots pine are the remains of Mains of Quirn. Follow the track through the wood to reach a signpost bearing the Speyside Way symbol. Turn right here Ⓒ to join this route following the sign to Ballindalloch.

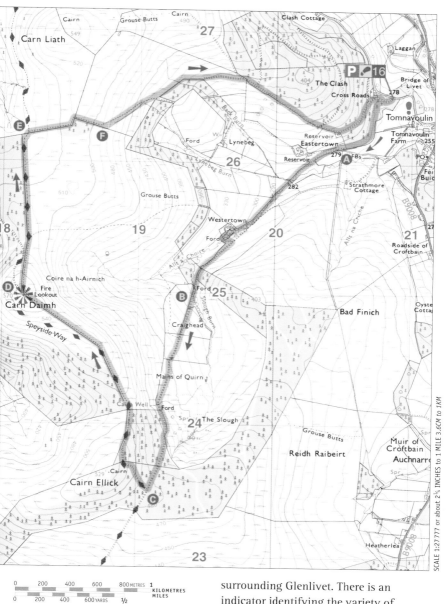

SCALE 1:27 777 or about 2½ INCHES to 1 MILE 3.6CM to 1KM

The path twists and turns through the forest, falling and rising, before it reaches a gate which gives on to open country. Follow the long track by the side of the plantation up to the summit of Carn Daimh **D** which is at 1,869ft (570m) and affords a glorious panorama of the countryside surrounding Glenlivet. There is an indicator identifying the variety of landmarks which you should be able to see from here on a good day.

From Carn Daimh take the track due north which follows the fence and drops down to a plantation. Here a path leaves to the right to Tomnavoulin via Westertown which could serve as a short cut if time is short. Continue northwards to the bottom corner of the plantation  **E** where the path turns to the east. After 100 yds the Speyside Way leaves to the left but our route keeps ahead, following the fence. The way through the heather gets easier to follow as you climb.

The path turns left at a corner of the fence by a lone, stunted Scots pine. After 100 yds turn right to follow a fence down towards Tomnavoulin. Before reaching a plantation the way swings left to go over a stile **F** then follow the narrow footpath downhill before turning right at a waymarker and heading towards the corner of a wood. Turn left along the edge of the wood then right when it ends and along the far side. When this ends a waymarker points to a faint path ahead leading to another wood. Cross a stile then continue along a track, downhill through Clash woods to return to the start.

Corryhabbie Hill and Glenlivet

A Walk around Loch Muick

Start	Spittal of Glenmuick	**GPS waypoints**	
Distance	7½ miles (12km)	 NO 309 851	
Height gain	230 feet (70m)	Ⓐ NO 303 841	
Approximate time	3½ hours	Ⓑ NO 295 844	
		Ⓒ NO 288 821	
Parking	Car park at the end of the road through Glen Muick from Ballater		
Ordnance Survey maps	Landranger 44 (Ballater & Glen Clova), Explorer OL53 (Lochnagar, Glen Muick & Glen Clova)		

There is little need for skills in wayfaring or map reading on this walk – once on the shore of the loch it is just a matter of walking with Loch Muick to the left. Its name may derive from the Gaelic and mean 'the loch of the swine', or alternatively it may come from the Norse 'myrkr' from which we get the word 'murky'. Queen Victoria preferred to think of it as 'the lake of sorrow' even though she and Prince Albert spent many happy days here.

Although the Scottish word 'spittal' is derived from 'hospital' it would be a mistake to think that sick people were once brought to the Spittal of Glenmuick to be healed. The hospice which was once situated here provided shelter for travellers who were trying to cross the dangerous mountain passes. Later it was used by drovers and it actually survived until the mid-19th century when railways began to provide speedier ways of transporting cattle.

Follow the track from the car park to the visitor centre where there is an exhibition about the 6,350 acre (2,570 ha) reserve. This part of the Glen Muick estate was amongst the land added to the Balmoral Estate by King George VI between 1947 and 1951. The reserve area was established in 1970 when the Estate set up the visitor centre and employed the first countryside ranger. Beyond the visitor centre a signpost points ahead to the direct route to Lochnagar. Bear left to follow the sign to Loch Muick. Keep on towards the loch when a track

Loch Muick

leaves to the left. This is the Capel Mounth, the ancient way to Glen Clova used by smugglers and rustlers as well as by units of Bonnie Prince Charlie's army en route to their defeat at Culloden.

About a mile along the path from the visitor centre, and 300 yds before a clump of trees, turn right Ⓐ on to a path going towards the north end of Loch Muick. This is a wide, well-made path which crosses a wooden bridge and passes a boat-house. After this it joins the main driveway Ⓑ along the northern shore of the loch which goes to Glas-allt-Shiel. Queen Victoria built this lodge after the death of Prince Albert as 'my first widow's house, not built by him or hallowed by his memory' and it became one of her favourite haunts. The walking is easy on this smooth track and the steep, dark slopes on the far side of the loch are always dramatic and sometimes seem almost menacing. Byron roamed these hills as a boy and it is easy to understand how memories of such scenery inspired his poetry. He wrote a splendid piece on Lochnagar and compared the English countryside unfavourably with that of Scotland.

When you reach the woods follow the drive towards the lodge following a waymarked route that leads to the lochside path.

Keep to the path which is closest to the shore and runs around the western end of Loch Muick. A path to the right goes up the glen to Dubh Loch, another place of austere beauty which Queen Victoria often visited. It was during one of her excursions, which took in the Glas Allt waterfall and Dubh Loch, that she learned of the death of the Duke of Wellington. This was in September 1852. There is a beach with golden sand which

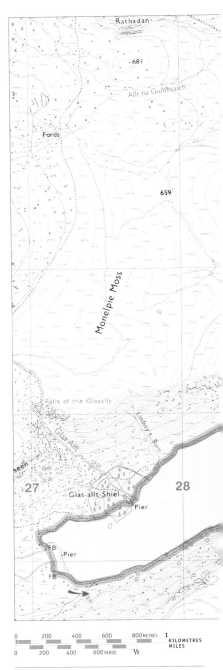

makes an ideal playground. This too was a spot loved by the Queen Victoria and was frequently used as the venue for royal picnics.

The return leg of the walk is by a

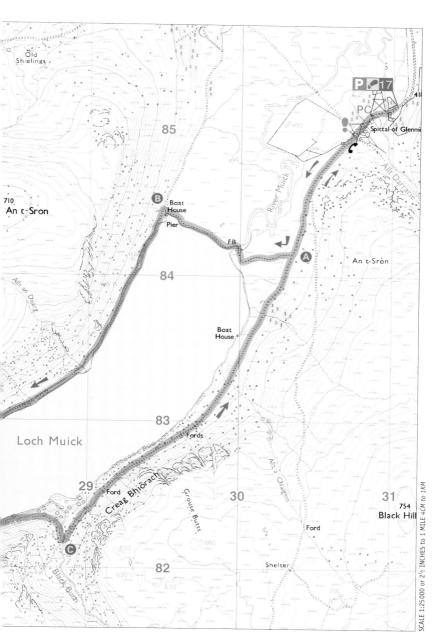

narrow path which clings to steep slopes clothed with birches, blaeberries and foxgloves. The birch trees are particularly beautiful as the path approaches the bridge over the Black Burn where it joins the track mentioned earlier coming from the Cairn Bannoch ridge **C**.

The final two miles or so by the side of the loch are comparatively unspectacular but the going is easy and the views ahead rewarding. After passing an isolated clump of trees the track leaves the lochside and soon returns to the visitor centre and the car park.
●

Eag a' Chait and Loch Morlich

		GPS waypoints	
Start	The bridge at the west end of Loch Morlich		NH 956 097
Distance	7¾ miles (12.3km)	**A**	NH 949 082
Height gain	1,015 feet (310m)	**B**	NH 952 067
		C	NH 963 065
Approximate time	4 hours	**D**	NH 968 064
Parking	Laneside at start	**E**	NH 966 075
		F	NH 974 083
Ordnance Survey maps	Landranger 36 (Grantown & Aviemore), Explorer OL57 (Cairn Gorm & Aviemore)	**G**	NH 977 088

The route provides a mixture of scenery with forestry plantings at first as the road gradually climbs to Rothiemurchus Lodge. This modern group of buildings is set in moorland dotted with clumps of old Scots pines. The path then climbs to the rocky pass of Eag a' Chait, giving grand views to the Cairngorm summits. However, just below the top of the pass the route turns northwards to head back to Loch Morlich, at first through a wonderful area of ancient forest (where you stand a chance of meeting reindeer) and then through plantings. The return is along forestry tracks above the southern side of the loch, which is relatively unfrequented but just as beautiful as the more popular shores.

Cross the bridge and walk up the track towards Rothiemurchus Lodge. The track is initially close to the shore and soon divides. Keep ahead to Lochan nan Geadas which is reached after about 15 minutes. This delightful little stretch of water is a secluded paradise for wildlife. There are good views of the hills ahead including the conical Castle Hill which rises to the south of Eag a' Chait. When the track divides **A** take the left fork and head towards Rothiemurchus Lodge.

Unfortunately, the path shown on the map which leaves the track shortly after this junction has been

lost so there is no alternative to following the track to the Lodge. The scenery changes at a cattle-grid where forestry plantings end. When you reach the Lodge walk through the complex, bearing to the right of the top building towards the helipad.

From here **B** the path is vague as it crosses boggy ground. Head east for the saddle between Airgiod-meall and Castle Hill. You can see the path ahead on the shoulder of the hill. Having skirted a hillock topped with a handful of Scots pines, the path crosses a final short stretch of boggy ground to a path climbing Coire Buidhe. The path becomes distinct as

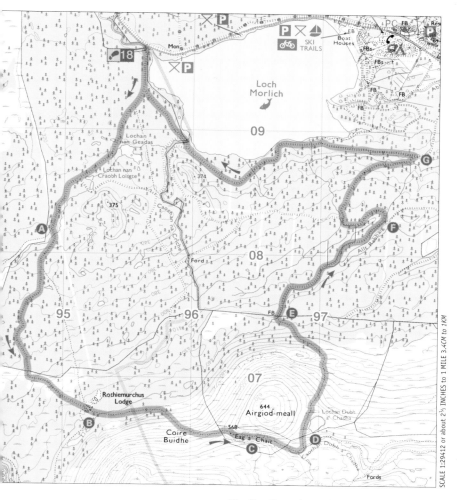

SCALE 1:29412 or about 2⅔ INCHES to 1 MILE 3.4CM to 1KM

it rises above tree level and a wide view opens up to Loch Morlich. The steepest part of the climb comes when the deer fence is reached, but this section is brief and you are soon in Eag a' Chait **C**.

The pass is filled with scattered boulders but these end just beyond the summit. Shortly after the boulders end look for a path to the left **D** which climbs to the deer fence. Walk by the side of the deer fence for about 150 yds to find steps over it. The path then skirts Lochan Dubh a'

Chadha. From here there is a spectacular view across the water to the summits, corries and plateau of the Cairngorm massif.

The path begins to descend with Loch Morlich ahead and the Kincardine Hills beyond. It is interesting to see Scots pine seedlings struggling to survive. This heads north to cross a dry valley and then descends through mature pines. It crosses a clearing with electricity poles and then comes to a forest hut locally known as Utsi's Hut after Mikel Utsi who re-introduced reindeer to the Cairngorms. On the other side of a lovely burn there is a gate giving on to a forest track **E**

Loch Morlich

and by it a notice: '*Dangifer Tarundas* Beware the Bulls', this with a painting of a reindeer. This area, including the part you have just walked through is a reindeer enclosure. *Signs advise you to stick to the paths.* During May and June the deer are calving and you should do nothing that might disturb them. In September and October it is rutting season and some bulls can become aggressive. The sign advises that you enter at your own risk. However you should not encounter any problems if you stick to the paths. Further information can be obtained from the Reindeer Co Ltd on tel. 01479 861228.

The track follows the stream which was crossed earlier. When the track divides at **F** turn left and proceed to the next junction of forest roads, which is in about 500 yds. Turn right here and continue for about $^1/_2$ mile to yet another junction of forest roads.

Turn left on to a broad track **G**, this track leads along the southern shore of Loch Morlich.

The broad sandy track gives views of the loch at first but soon leaves it. You will still be following red-topped posts but bear right to leave them when they lead to the left. Cross a stile into the Rothiemurchus Estate and follow the good sandy path which gives views across the loch, with windsurfers providing colour and action. At a T-junction turn right to retrace your steps to the bridge at the start. ●

Loch an Eilein

		GPS waypoints
Start	Coylum Bridge	🖉 NH 914 106
Distance	8 miles (12.9km)	Ⓐ NH 917 100
Height gain	425 feet (130m)	Ⓑ NH 925 078
Approximate time	4 hours	Ⓒ NH 916 079
Parking	Layby on south side of B970 just before campsite and bridge	Ⓓ NH 905 077
		Ⓔ NH 897 086
Ordnance Survey maps	Landranger 36 (Grantown & Aviemore), Explorer OL57 (Cairn Gorm & Aviemore)	Ⓕ NH 905 100

The lack of any severe gradients on this walk will appeal to many and, although flat, the route has much to offer in the way of fine scenery. It starts by the Coylum Bridge campsite at the beginning of the Lairig Ghru, the long distance path which leads over the mountains to Braemar. This takes you to the Cairngorm Club footbridge where there is a choice of burnside picnic sites, some with sandy beaches. Then the way is westwards through ancient Scots pines and past beautiful lochans to Loch an Eilein. Most people arrive at this popular beauty spot by car and do not venture as far as its western shores so you should be able to enjoy peaceful walking along the paths away from the car park. The return to Coylum Bridge is on estate roads and footpaths through more of the beautiful and fragrant Rothiemurchus pine forest.

🖉 The start of the Lairig Ghru is marked on the main road by a green signpost. The track passes the campsite and even here the character of the Rothiemurchus forest is apparent with its beautiful old Scots pines. Keep a lookout for red squirrels on this walk: if you have a dog it will alert you to their presence in the boughs above, and you may see the remains of neatly nibbled pine cones. Pass Lairig Ghru Cottage on an excellent level path which follows the stream, 100 yds or so away from its bank. In about ¹/₂ mile bear left when the path divides Ⓐ. The other path is signed to Gleann Eanaich. After a stile over a

Beautiful Lochan Deò

wall the path crosses a burn and becomes narrow with banks of heather on each side. The sound of rushing water increases as you approach a gate and from here there is a view of the mountains ahead, with the notch that the Lairig Ghru passes through clearly visible. A short distance farther on a track leaves to the right **B** but continue to the river and to the Cairngorm Club footbridge where, if you wish, you can explore a little further to find quiet picnic places by the river, often with sandy beaches which will appeal to youngsters.

Return to **B** and fork left following the sign to Loch an Eilein. The track crosses an attractive heather-covered heath scattered with Scots pines. There is a fine view back from this enjoyable section of the walk. The lovely little Lochan Deò is on the left just before the path comes to a cross-ways **C**. Keep ahead here and cross two sparkling burns by footbridges. Loch an Eilein comes into view soon after this in its woodland setting.

Turn left when you come to the T-junction **D** above the eastern shore of the loch. *If you wish you can shorten the route by turning right here.* Pass a bench sited by a large stone and follow the path in a clockwise direction around the loch. Sometimes the path is close to the

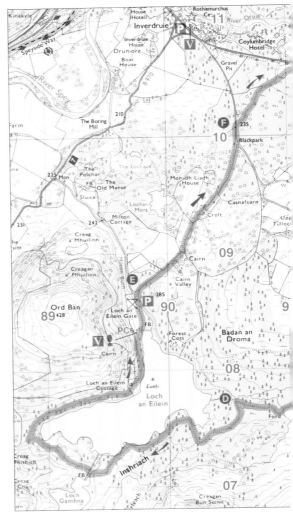

water, often it is at some distance. The loch seems to grow in size as you walk westwards. At the head of the loch there is a wooden bridge which gives a view of the neighbouring Loch Gamhna. Another in a series of well situated seats is nearby and a path goes off left round Kennapole Hill which is crowned by a memorial cairn to a Duchess of Bedford.

Within about 20 minutes you pass Loch an Eilein Cottage, where the

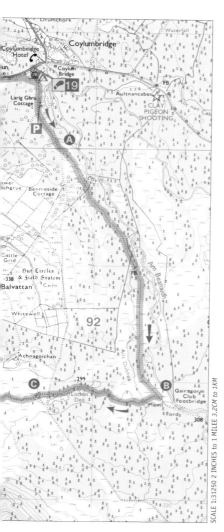

In 1690 the castle was besieged by a group of Jacobites retreating after their defeat at the Battle of Cromdale. The defence was led by a formidable lady, Dame Grizel Mor Grant, who was the widow of the fifth laird Grant and who supervised the casting of ammunition for her garrison. At this time the castle was connected to the shore by an easily defended zigzag causeway but this was lost when the level of the loch was raised in the 18th century. If you shout vigorously across the loch you may hear a unique triple echo as your voice is bounced to and fro from the crumbling walls of the castle to the tree-covered hillsides.

From the castle it is only a short step to the car park, a good place to be at about 6pm when weary walkers and mountain-bikers limp in from excursions over the Lairig Ghru. Pass the car park on the left then cross a bridge and turn right 100 yds beyond **E** on to a track with a notice which requests 'Estate vehicles only please'. There are times when you can catch a glimpse of Lochan Mor (better known as the 'Lily Loch') through trees to the left before passing cottages to the right and a big house, Monadh Liadh, to the left.

The very pleasant track joins a surfaced road at Blackpark. Keep straight on but within 200 yds turn right **F** on to a footpath which crosses the road. This grassy path is an enjoyable finale to the walk as it leads through Scots pines and divides opposite the entrance to Coylumbridge Resort Hotel. At this point take the right fork to continue walking parallel to the road and you will eventually reach the Lairig Ghru track by a gate. Turn left here to reach the B970 at Coylum Bridge and the layby from which you set off. ●

loch is fringed with cherry trees, and immediately after this comes the castle itself. This was a stronghold of Alexander Stewart, Earl of Buchan, the bastard son of King Robert II, who was given the name of 'the Wolf of Badenoch' from the savagery of his bitter feud with the clergy which resulted in his being excommunicated. This was after he had put the town of Forres to the torch and burned down the cathedral at Elgin. He died in about 1405 and achieved an undeserved fame by being made the swash-buckling hero of a Victorian novel.

Fiacaill and Cairn Lochan

		GPS waypoints
Start	Coire Cas car park	
Distance	6½ miles (10.5km)	🖉 NH 989 061
Height gain	2,625 feet (800m)	Ⓐ NH 995 049
		Ⓑ NH 998 039
Approximate time	5 hours	Ⓒ NH 991 027
Parking	Car park at the top of the Ski	Ⓓ NH 985 025
	Road	Ⓔ NH 979 044
Ordnance Survey maps	Landranger 36 (Grantown & Aviemore), Explorer OL57 (Cairn Gorm & Aviemore)	

It would be foolish to pretend that the climb to the Cairngorm plateau via the Fiacaill ridge is an easy one. However, there is much satisfaction in climbing to the rim of Coire an t-Sneachda, and after reaching the midway point of the funicular neither this, nor the ski tows, intrude on the scenery. The traverse of two of the most spectacular Cairngorm corries is exciting. However, this walk is not one to undertake in the mist as, not only would spectacular views be missed, but expert navigation would be required.

🖉 Walk up the path which passes to the left of the bottom chairlift station and then climb up the service road which leads to the midway station. This will take about 15 minutes and is the most tedious part of the ascent. Keep to the main path which passes beneath the cables just before the first disembarkation point. After the station the broad track climbs steeply and makes a sharp left-hand bend. Look for the path to the right Ⓐ which leaves the summit path here and is signposted to Fiacaill. A flight of stone steps takes the path up from the main track.

The climb is steep but enjoyable and much effort has been spent in keeping the path in good repair. Keep to the centre of the path to avoid damaging the delicate vegetation on either side. As you near the top the path becomes rather more diffuse and

there are wonderful views from the narrowing buttress of Coire Cas to the left and the dark crags of Coire an t-Sneachda to the right. At last the large cairn Ⓑ comes into view. It will have taken you about an hour to reach this from the car park.

Walk around the edge of Coire an t-Sneachda following the cairns. It is easy to think that the way might be less difficult if you took to less stony ground to the left. This would be a mistake: you would not only increase the distance but the stupendous views northwards, framed by crags and pinnacles, would be missed.

At the western side of Coire an t-Sneachda the well trodden path to Ben Macdui strikes southwards (to the left) Ⓒ. Instead of taking this

0	200	400	600	800 METRES	1	
						KILOMETRES
						MILES
0	200	400	600 YARDS	½		

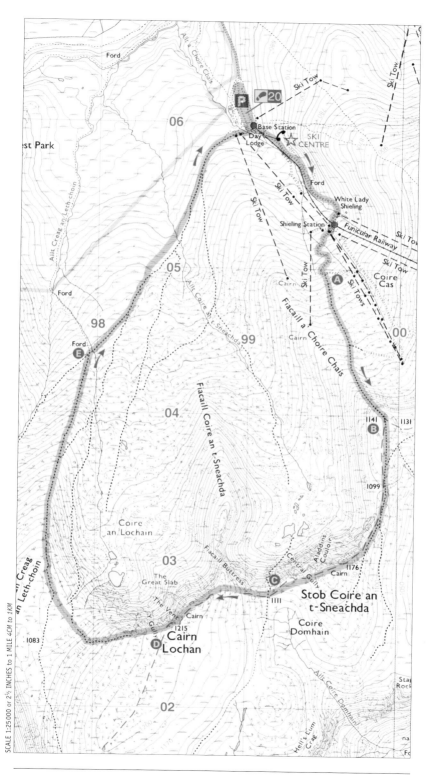

SCALE 1:25 000 or 2½ INCHES to 1 MILE 4CM to 1KM

Loch Morlich from Coire an t-Sneachda

path, however, take the lesser one ahead following cairns by the edge of Fiacaill Buttress and enjoying stupendous views northwards. On a good day you will be able to see the Sutherland mountains clearly and some have claimed to see the Cuillins of Skye from the Cairngorm summits. There is a cairn at the top of the buttress which is probably the best viewpoint on this route. Look to the left beyond the lochans on the floor of Coire an Lochain to see the homeward path.

A series of small cairns leads you around the rim of the corrie and up to the summit of Cairn Lochan **D** where the cairn itself (at 3,986ft/1,215m) is built very close to the edge of a sheer drop of 1,000ft (300m) – a fact made all the more dramatic by the rock towers which overlook it. It is also worth looking southwards for a view of Ben Macdui, whose cairn should be quite clearly visible.

Leave the cairn and follow the rim of Coire an Lochain gradually turning towards the north-west and still following cairns. Keep Coire an Lochain on your right and descend the easy ridge to the ford **E**. Continue to the second ford at the crossing of the Allt Coire an t-Sneachda. Many people come this far from the car park – it is just a few minutes walk from here to the starting point. ●

Morrone

Start	The Duck Pond, Braemar (take the Linn of Dee road but fork left at Airlie House and climb to the end of the road, Chapel Brae)	GPS waypoints
		NO 143 910
		Ⓐ NO 144 904
		Ⓑ NO 132 886
		Ⓒ NO 152 882
		Ⓓ NO 149 904
Distance	7 miles (11.3km)	
Height gain	2,015 feet (615m)	
Approximate time	4 hours	
Parking	Car park at start	
Ordnance Survey maps	Landranger 43 (Braemar & Blair Atholl), Explorer OL52 (Glen Shee & Braemar)	

At 2,815ft (859m) Morrone ('the big nose') is a fair way from being a Munro, yet it is still a considerable hill if only in terms of its bulk. It lies to the south of Braemar, a whaleback crowned with a radio mast which makes it unmistakable both from the village and more remote points such as the Linn of Quoich. In fact, on this route you only have to climb a little over 1,600ft (490m) to the summit which is an excellent viewpoint for much of Deeside, Lochnagar and other major peaks of the Cairngorms. Note that if you take dogs on this walk you may have to lift them over the high stile at Ⓓ.

The walk starts from the large car park by the duck pond at the end of Chapel Brae on the west side of Braemar. This is part of the village of Auchendryne which was originally separate from Castleton on the east side of the River Dee. The two places joined to establish Braemar ('the Brae of Mar') when royalty made the district popular. Walk past the pond on the track and bear left when this divides following a blue waymark.

The going becomes quite steep as the track passes a cottage (Woodhill). Bear left again after this and climb to a seat and a mountain indicator. The view takes in many of the peaks surrounding Braemar, the most notable being Ben Macdui and Braeriach to the north-west. Some of the mountains shown on the indicator are not actually visible since it was designed to stand in a position about 55ft higher! This is a part of the Morrone Birkwood Nature Reserve and there is a noticeboard describing the wildlife that may be seen on the hill. It is claimed that this is the finest example of upland birchwood to be found in Britain. Geologically, Morrone is mainly of quartzite though there is also an outcrop of limestone.

Continue for 100 yds beyond the indicator and then take the path to the right Ⓐ clearly marked first by a post and then by a cairn. The path climbs steadily and it is as well to pause occasionally to catch breath and take in the views to Braemar. The

SCALE 1:27777 or about 2¼ INCHES to 1 MILE 3.6CM to 1KM

Scale bar:
```
0   200   400   600   800 METRES  1
                                   KILOMETRES
                                   MILES
0   200   400   600 YARDS  ½
```

village is situated at a height of over 1,000ft (305m) and is amongst the highest in Scotland. This altitude, combined with the surrounding hills which trap cold air, have bestowed on Braemar the unenviable record of having experienced the lowest temperature ever recorded in Britain, the -28°C (-18°F) which was reached in January 1982.

The vistas are even better after climbing beyond a deer fence with the famous Games Park clearly visible – this is where the Highland Gathering is held on the first weekend in September each year. The path strikes southwards up the broad shoulder of the hill and Braemar Castle appears neatly framed in a cleft of tree-clad hills. You may think that you are almost at the top when you reach a line of four cairns which might have once served as shooting butts. However, the summit is still about another ½ mile ahead, though the worst of the climbing is now at an end.

The summit itself  is bare, the only feature being the radio mast and the paraphernalia around it. Part of this is a weather recording centre, the readings from which are relayed to a noticeboard in Braemar village centre by the post office. By now Braemar is out of sight and the interest lies in attempting to identify the surrounding peaks.

Ben Avon with its distinctive tors is obvious to the north with Beinn a' Bhuird to the left, a more anonymous, broad-topped hill. Turning to the right there is a grand view down the River Dee with the magnificent face of Lochnagar overlooking it farther to the east. Loch Callater is obvious to the south-east and its glen is followed by the famous Jock's Road via Fafernie and Tolmount, and then on into Glen Clova. To the south the shape of Cairnwell is unmistakable, while the climax of the scene comes with the major peaks of the Cairngorms arrayed to the north-west.

Walk past the radio mast to the Land Rover track on the other side. This can be seen winding southwards over the hill. You will probably see more grouse on this hill (where they are protected) than on any of its neighbours.

Although the way is long it is never dreary with different views opening up all the time. When you reach the road  turn left and walk by the Clunie Water to pass through the golf course. At the end of this, just before a cattle-grid, turn left  and climb up steeply by a small caravan site to a deer fence (a dog would need to be exceptionally agile to climb the steps here). After crossing this take the path which still climbs, winding through a birch wood to a second fence. Here the path leaves the birches and there is an abandoned house to the right (Tomintoul). The path joins a track which leads past the path going up to Morrone  and the mountain indicator encountered earlier. From here retrace your steps past Woodhill to return to the duck pond. ●

Braemar from Morrone

Cambus o' May and the Muir of Dinnet

		GPS waypoints
Start	Dinnet, 6 miles west of Aboyne where the A97 crosses the A93	✏ NO 459 987
Distance	9¼ miles (14.9km)	Ⓐ NO 456 996
Height gain	445 feet (135m)	Ⓑ NO 450 994
Approximate time	4½ hours	Ⓒ NO 448 998
Parking	Car park at Dinnet crossroads	Ⓓ NJ 434 009
Ordnance Survey maps	Landrangers 37 (Strathdon & Alford) and 44 (Ballater & Glen Clova), Explorer OL54 (Glen Esk & Glen Tanor)	Ⓔ NO 406 980
		Ⓕ NO 421 976

There are at least three contrasting landscapes to be enjoyed on this lengthy walk. First you pass through the flat landscape surrounding lochs Kinord and Davan, part of a nature reserve where birdwatchers will be in their element. These lochs are shallow and owe their origin to glacial deposits unlike the far deeper ones which nestle below Cairngorm peaks and were formed by glacial erosion. Later the route climbs the flank of Culblean Hill with its Scots pines and silver birches before descending through forest to the disused railway line along wooded banks of the River Dee. Try to find time to visit the Burn o' Vat while you are here. The short walk will only take 30 minutes or so.

✏ From the car park in the centre of Dinnet walk northwards on the A97 for about ½ mile before turning left Ⓐ on to a track into the Muir of Dinnet National Nature Reserve. *Note that the Nature Reserve bylaws require dogs to be on leads at all times in order to protect ground-nesting birds.*

The track crosses heathland before coming to the old schoolhouse which formerly served Dinnet even though it was about one mile from the village. School children used a more direct path but even so they often had to battle to their lessons through

snow or driving rain. Turn right at the junction by the school Ⓑ on to the track which leads to the Warden's House at New Kinord.

Turn left at another T-junction Ⓒ to pass the house and continue through meadows which give pastoral views of Loch Kinord to the left. A Bronze Age crannog (a settlement on an artificial island) lies just offshore. Bear left and go through a metal gate where this track divides. It turns northwards away from the shore and the ruins of Old Kinord can be seen to the right. Bear left when the track from the old croft joins the path and cross beneath electricity cables, the first of several occasions on this walk when they provide a useful landmark. Loch Davan will now be seen to the right before trees hide it as the track wanders through birches and eventually reaches the main road. These shallow lochs are a haven for birdlife and are typical of those to be found in areas where, at the end of the last Ice Age, glaciers deposited their load of debris. Scottish Natural Heritage manage the site for a variety of water birds.

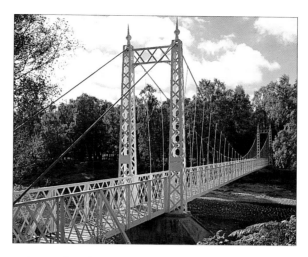

Cambus o' May bridge

Eventually emerging onto a road bear right and follow it about 400 yds to a road junction ⒟ where the road to Raebush goes ahead and leaves the B9119. Turn left here to take a track which divides after 50 yds. Take the lesser track here to the left which passes through woods at first before climbing on to the heather-covered hill. This is Culblean Hill where the Battle of Culblean was fought in 1335 – a significant victory for the Scots under Sir Andrew de Moray over the English troops of the Earl of Atholl (who died on the battlefield). Culblean marked the turning point in the Second Scottish War of Independence which kept the 11-year-old King David II on the Scottish throne – though the King himself actually lived safely in France throughout the campaign.

The path climbs steadily passing beneath powerlines again. Young pine trees growing in the middle of the track show how quickly the way could become lost. Eventually the climbing ends and the valley of the Vat Burn is to the left as more power lines come into view. The track descends to ford the little Vat Burn, then comes to a Muir of Dinnet National Nature Reserve noticeboard. You leave the reserve at this point to enter Forest Enterprise land.

The track soon heads southwards through the forest. Bear left when it divides following a yellow waymark. At a cattle-grid the forest walks are waymarked off to the right but this route crosses the grid and remains on the track. It reaches the main road close to The Cranach coffee shop (right). Cross the road to the trackbed of the old railway ⒠ which now serves as a footpath and cycle track. Turn left and enjoy the level walking on a good surface. This is one of the finest sections of the walk with the river on your right as you pass the elegant Cambus o' May suspension bridge ⒡ and then the former station, now restored to serve as a private dwelling.

After the station the old railway

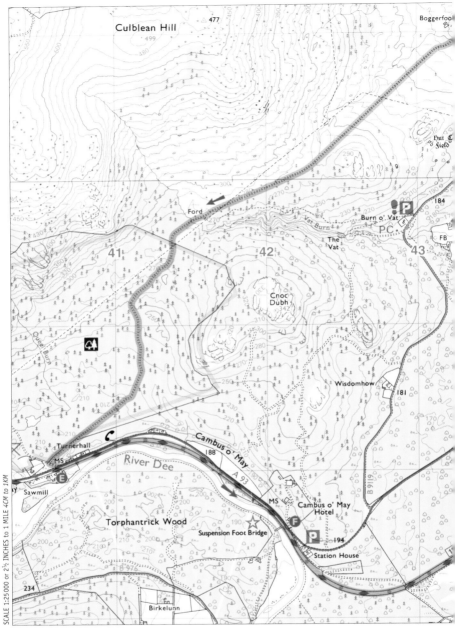

SCALE 1:25000 or 2½ INCHES to 1 MILE 4CM to 1KM

leaves the river and, after a bridge, runs in an almost straight line for nearly two miles. There is a steady climb at first and one can easily imagine the fireman's anxiety in the days of steam as he tried to keep a good fire burning from Cambus o' May. The hills are vaguely seen through the birches to the right and there is also a fine view back towards the Cairngorms. As you near Dinnet

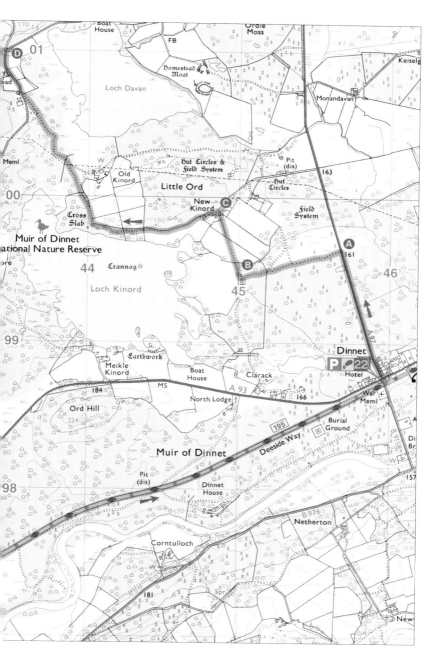

the way passes through the heart of the Muir of Dinnet, a wide glacial basin overlooked by fine hills where the birch scrub and heather are particularly attractive in late summer and autumn. Dinnet itself was a village which sprang from the coming of the railway. Its only other claim to fame was that, at the age of eight, Lord Byron spent time at a nearby farm recovering from scarlet fever. The former railway brings you back to the centre of the village opposite the starting point.

Gleann Eanaich

Start	On the lane from Inverdruie about ¼ mile before Whitewell
Distance	13 miles (20.8km)
Height gain	985 feet (300m)
Approximate time	6½ hours
Parking	Layby and verge parking at the start
Ordnance Survey maps	Landranger 36 (Grantown & Aviemore), Explorer OL57 (Cairn Gorm & Aviemore)

GPS waypoints

- NH 914 090
- Ⓐ NH 916 079
- Ⓑ NH 928 065
- Ⓒ NH 929 055
- Ⓓ NH 924 048
- Ⓔ NH 925 029
- Ⓕ NH 920 001
- Ⓖ NN 916 998

This is a long walk into the heart of the western Cairngorms through the Rothiemurchus pine forest and one of the finest glens to Loch Eanaich. Navigation is straightforward as the route lies on paths and tracks. However, the higher section beyond the forest has no shelter in bad weather and, after heavy rain or rapid thaw, some of the burn crossings may be difficult. Also snow can lie very deep here well into spring, hiding the path. In such conditions it would be inadvisable to venture beyond point Ⓓ.

Take the vehicle track from the layby, curving to the right and descend to the track coming from Coylumbridge. Turn right on to this and follow it for ½ mile to a crossways Ⓐ. Keep ahead here, following the sign to Loch Eanaich (Einich) and with the attractive Lochan Deò to the left. After roughly 100 yds pass through a gate which is also marked to Loch Eanaich at a point where a track comes in from the right. To the left the scattered mature Scots pines have abundant young trees below them. These are self sown trees and are the natural continuation of the 8000-year-old forest. About ¾ mile farther on the first of half a dozen or so burns crosses the path.

At Ⓑ cross another burn and continue ahead following the sign

'Footpath and Cyclists'. A steep track goes off to the right here. On the left a striking row of dead pines overlooks the burn. For a while beyond this point the path runs almost level along the east-facing side of a steep slope. The pines to the left are exceptionally fine with both wet and dry areas beneath them, hummocky ground supporting bracken and blaeberries. The occasional large dead pine is a vital part of the forest habitat; crested tits, special birds of the pine forest, will only nest in such trees. Their spluttering trill can often be heard along this section of the route. Am Beanaidh, the river flowing from Loch Eanaich, can be heard rushing down the glen. Directly ahead the cone of Carn Eilrig fills the view with pines reaching high up its slopes.

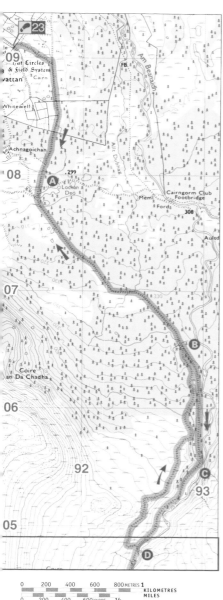

The path turns a sharp corner at **C**. Ahead the forest is suddenly reduced to the narrow confines of the burn while beyond is the first glimpse of open country. Continue to **D** where the track which left the route at **B** rejoins. Here are the last few pines of

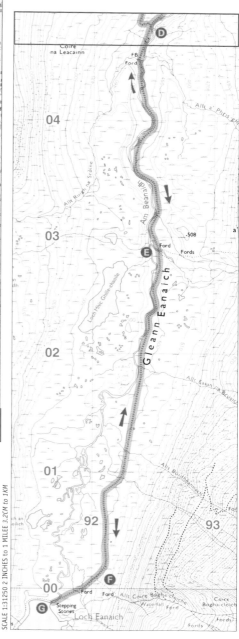

Where Am Beanaidh comes into view there is a fine stand of alders and rowan growing around an island in the river. Beyond, the pinewood rises to blend into a solid mass of deep blue-green. In one place the path crosses a steep loose slope of exposed sands and gravels left by the ice sheet as it melted thousands of years ago.

SCALE 1:31250 2 INCHES to 1 MILEE 3.2CM to 1KM

the forest. Tradition has it that, in the spring, cattle used to be driven to this point and would then make their own way up Gleann Eanaich for the summer, to be followed later by the herdsmen and their families who lived in shielings (rough huts) in the glen throughout the summer. In the far distance steep ridges and cliffs below Sgoran Dubh Mór can be seen.

Continue southwards along the track and in about 500 yds cross a footbridge over Am Beanaidh.

At **E** you have to ford the Beanaidh Bheag which is a sizeable burn draining the high corries of Braeriach. It may well be necessary to detour upstream to find a crossing place. In spate it may not be possible to cross and you will be forced to turn back. Ahead Gleann Eanaich is dramatic with the mountains closing in. The route south finally leaves the confines of the glacial terraces and runs in a straight line over gently undulating ground. In autumn red deer congregate here, the hoarse bellowing of the stags echoing from the hills. By staying on the track you will be able to watch them without causing any disturbance.

Gleann Eanaich

Loch Eanaich finally comes into view as a sliver of silver at the head of the glen. On the right the cliffs and gullies below Sgoran Dubh and Sgor Gaoith can be seen. In the early part of this century these cliffs were popular with Cairngorm mountaineers but in recent decades they have fallen out of favour, other steeper cliffs at higher altitudes providing greater challenges. The track detours left to avoid an extensive area of peat bog. Hundreds of pine stumps and roots can be seen here. These are several thousand years old and show the height at which the trees thrived formerly before the climate became cooler and wetter, and peat prevented the growth of young trees.

At **F** a tumbledown cairn marks the point at which an old stalkers' path branches off to the left. If you climb a little way up this path you will see a fine series of waterfalls, though beyond this the path climbs high into the hills and is only a route for the experienced and well-equipped walker.

Continuing on the main track you finally reach Loch Eanaich **G**. About 1 ½ miles long, the loch provides the main drinking supply for Strathspey. The water here is clear because of the very low level of nutrients,which is the result of rainwater draining off the surrounding hills of bare granite. The cliffs at the head of the loch are an important site for some of the less common Cairngorm flowers and scrub willows.

The return to Whitewell is by the same route, though at **D** you should follow the track up to the left if you want to get the best views back up the glen. This path rejoins the outward route at **B**. The descent into the shelter of the pine forest makes a fine end to a long day. ●

Bynack More from Glenmore

		GPS waypoints	
Start	Allt Mor car park		NH 983 087
Distance	14¼ miles (23km)	Ⓐ	NH 991 090
Height gain	2,625 feet (800m)	Ⓑ	NH 992 097
Approximate time	7½ hours	Ⓒ	NJ 020 105
Parking	Free parking at start	Ⓓ	NJ 039 080
Ordnance Survey maps	Landranger 36 (Grantown & Aviemore), Explorer OL57 (Cairn Gorm & Aviemore)	Ⓔ	NJ 037 066

The approach and walk out is on well defined forest roads. However, the ascent and descent of Bynack More is a demanding hill walk on a rough path and open moor. The final half mile to the summit traverses a fine ridge which is interesting but without any difficulties in summer. The summit reveals splendid views over Loch Avon and the central Cairngorm Mountains.
This is a strenuous walk, which should only be attempted in good weather.

From the Allt Mor car park head off in a south-easterly direction indicated by a purple marker post. Almost immediately cross the narrow timber footbridge over the Allt Mor. (The footbridge can be seen from the car park.) After crossing the bridge turn left, the path soon becomes a forest road.

After about 500 yds another forest road goes left, keep straight on here, all tracks are indicated with purple marker posts. A metal 'Bailey' bridge over the Alt na Ciste is crossed.

At Ⓐ the track divides to form a turning loop for forestry vehicles. Turn right, pass the purple marker post, and soon turn right again onto a path by another purple marker. This path passes over a footbridge in order to avoid the ford across the Allt Ban.

After the bridge the path joins a forest road, turn left, then immediately right to rejoin the main track. Another purple marker post confirms the way.

At Ⓑ turn right. You now follow blue markers to Lochan Uaine, the Green Lochan. This beautiful lochan takes its colour from the surrounding Scots Pine woodland. Rest awhile here on your return. Follow the main track past the lochan and turn right at the fork in about 400 yds. Note the views over Loch a Gharbh-choire towards Abernethy Forest.

The track becomes rough and wet on the approach to Ⓒ Bynack Stable. Cross the bridge over the River Nethy and commence the steady climb up the obvious but rough path ahead. This path leads eventually to the

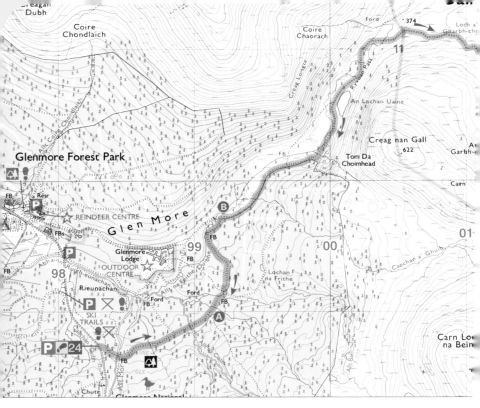

Lairig an Laoigh, a route right through the Cairngorm mountains to rival the better known Lairig Ghru.

Bynack More

The path levels out and divides. Both become vague. The Lairig an Laoigh path swings away to the east and starts to descend. Our path crosses spot height 818m (2,683ft) **D** from which the main ridge of Bynack More rises dead ahead. The first few feet of the ridge is up steep grass after which the gradient eases. The ridge is boulder strewn on the right and rocky on the left. The crest is not sharp and provides an interesting and relatively safe route to the top. At last the summit

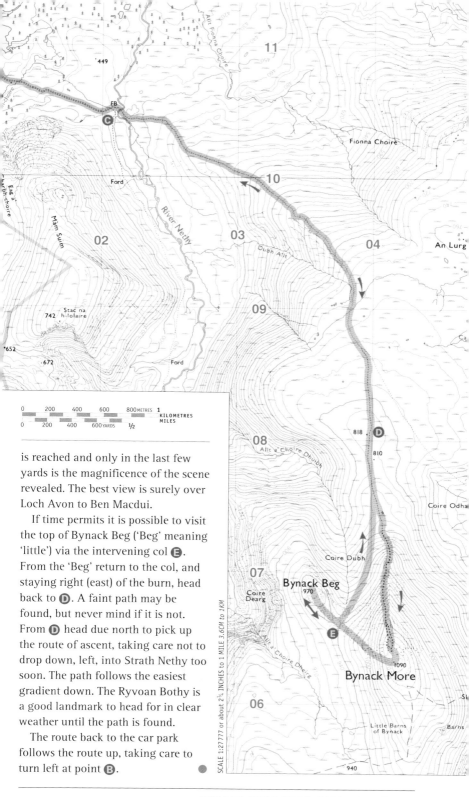

is reached and only in the last few yards is the magnificence of the scene revealed. The best view is surely over Loch Avon to Ben Macdui.

If time permits it is possible to visit the top of Bynack Beg ('Beg' meaning 'little') via the intervening col **E**. From the 'Beg' return to the col, and staying right (east) of the burn, head back to **D**. A faint path may be found, but never mind if it is not. From **D** head due north to pick up the route of ascent, taking care not to drop down, left, into Strath Nethy too soon. The path follows the easiest gradient down. The Ryvoan Bothy is a good landmark to head for in clear weather until the path is found.

The route back to the car park follows the route up, taking care to turn left at point **B**.

SCALE 1:27,777 or about 2½ INCHES to 1 MILE 3.6CM to 1KM

Carn an Fhreiceadain from Kingussie

Carn an Fhreiceadain from Kingussie

Start	Kingussie
Distance	10½ miles (17km)
Height gain	2,280 feet (695m)
Approximate time	5½ hours
Parking	Kingussie central car park
Ordnance Survey maps	Landranger 35 (Kingussie & Monadhliath Mountains), Explorer OL56 (Badenoch & Upper Strathspey)

GPS waypoints

- NH 755 007
- Ⓐ NH 749 029
- Ⓑ NH 744 056
- Ⓒ NH 739 069
- Ⓓ NH 725 071
- Ⓔ NH 733 050

Most of this walk is on well-defined tracks, though there is rough walking across heather for about one mile as you begin the descent from Carn an Fhreiceadain. The walk is a good introduction to the Monadhliath Mountains which lie to the west of the A9, an area neglected by many in favour of the popular Cairngorm routes. Although these summits lack the splendour of those to the east they provide fine viewpoints and you are unlikely to encounter anyone else in the course of the walk in this desolate but beautiful wilderness. In the shooting season ring 01540 661237 to make certain of safe access.

Turn left out of the car park entrance and walk up Gynack Road. Soon after passing the hospital (left) look for a fingerpost (right) and take the path to cross a footbridge over the Gynack Burn. The surfaced track continues to climb beyond the top of the golf course but ends at a bridge Ⓐ by a large cream coloured building with a curved roof. Do not cross the bridge but turn right up the track which follows the burn.

The plantations end and the track passes through a gate. Another gate takes the track on to the open hill. Already there is a fine view back with Creag Bheag well seen to the south as you climb higher. This is the peak to the south of Loch Gynack, not the lesser hill with the same name immediately to the east of the track. Creag Mhór is the rugged summit to the right as you look back with Creag Dhubh the higher peak a little way to the north. 'Creag Dhubh' is the battle-cry of the Clan Macpherson but it refers to the hill of the same name which rises to the south-west and overlooks Cluny Castle, once the headquarters of the clan. There is an abundance of foxgloves and juniper bushes by the track whose purpose is made clear as the first of a series of grouse butts comes into view. The sheep on this hill are a distinctive

0	200	400	600	800 METRES	1 KILOMETRES
0	200	400	600 YARDS	½	MILES

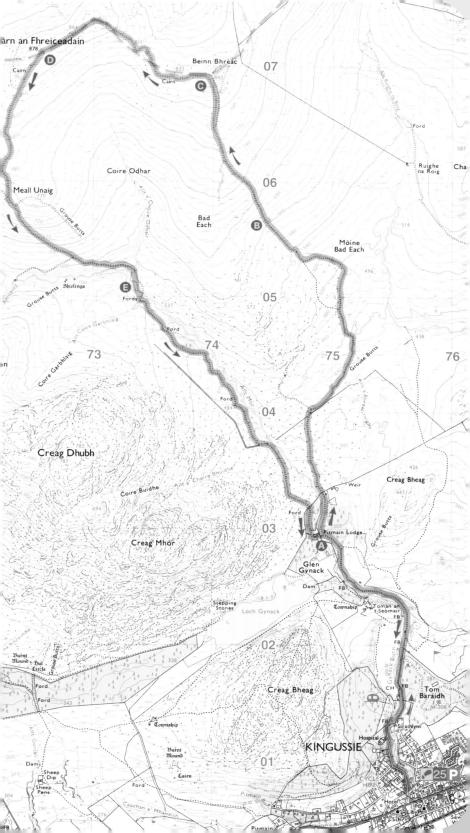

The track to Beinn Bhreac

breed which look as though they have goat genes in their ancestry.

The gradient becomes severe after the track runs past a wooden hut **B** but then eases off a little near the summit of Beinn Bhreac the next objective **C**.

From Beinn Bhreac head west on the path towards the cairn which is slightly lower than the summit. It is a wonderful viewpoint over miles of barren hills to the west while the majestic peaks of the Cairngorms are well seen to the north-east. From here walk one mile or so north-westwards on a well maintained track to the neighbouring summit of Carn an Fhreiceadain (2,880ft/878m) which has a triangulation pillar and a very distinctive cairn, both of which are usually visible on the skyline, the latter **D** being some distance farther on to the south-west. The name of the hill reflects its excellence as a viewpoint – translated from the Gaelic it means 'the lookout cairn'.

The Monadhliaths ('grey mountains') form part of the southern Grampians but contrast with the Cairngorms which also belong to this group and face them across the valley of the Spey. Where the latter are steep-sided and craggy the Monadhliath peaks are comparatively low and uniform with rare outcrops of rock. Few paths other than stalkers' tracks penetrate Byron's 'irksome solitudes' and thus they remain unexplored by most walkers.

From **D** the track follows the ridge southwards for ³/₄ mile to descend to Meall Unaig. From here descend the slopes to join the track by Allt Unaig which is more substantial after a bridge **E** where it becomes the Allt Mór.

The way back from here to Glen Gynack is very enjoyable. Follow the track all the way to Pitmain Lodge then cross the bridge at **A**. From here continue on the outward track to return to the footbridge over Gynack Burn, over which turn left down Gynack Road to the start. ●

Sron na Lairige and Braeriach from Loch an Eilein

		GPS waypoints
Start	Loch an Eilein	🖊 NH 897 085
Distance	18 miles (28.9km)	Ⓐ NH 905 077
Height gain	3,410 feet (1,040m)	Ⓑ NH 914 078
Approximate time	10 hours	Ⓒ NH 927 078
Parking	Car park at the head of the road	Ⓓ NH 938 075
Ordnance Survey maps	Landranger 36 (Grantown & Aviemore), Explorer OL57 (Cairn Gorm & Aviemore)	Ⓔ NH 958 037
		Ⓕ NN 952 998

This is a long and arduous walk, which should only be attempted in favourable summer conditions, and with an early start. *It features the traditional Cairngorm 'long walk in' giving a feeling of commitment and remoteness to the walk. The approach is through beautiful open Scots Pine forest, which gives way to the heavily glaciated northern end of the Lairig Ghru. The real climbing starts some six miles into the walk, up the northern slopes of Sron na Lairige. The walk may be terminated on this first summit, reducing the distance by a couple of miles.* Be prepared to turn back at any point, do not over extend yourself, and keep an eye on the time!

IMPORTANT NOTE! – Older maps may show the Sinclair Memorial Hut at the start of the Lairig Ghru. This has been demolished and there is no shelter here.

🖊 From Loch an Eilein car park head out the way you drove in, cross the bridge and turn immediately right, signposted 'Public Footpath to Braemar by the Lairig Ghru'. Continue above the north-eastern shore of the loch.

A footbridge Ⓐ is reached 10 yds before a junction. Turn left here signposted 'Lairig Ghru and Gleann Eanaich'. The next two fords are bridged. Here we pass through some of the most beautiful Scots Pine woodland in Scotland with views to Cairngorm and Cairn Lochan ahead.

At Ⓑ a fork in the path is reached. Keep left as signposted 'Cyclists'. After 50 yds the path forks again, keep right. After 30 yds there is a crossroads of paths, go straight on (the main Gleann Eanaich track is visible from here). After a further 75 yds the main Gleann Eanaich track is reached, go straight across into the trees, signposted Lairig Ghru. (The

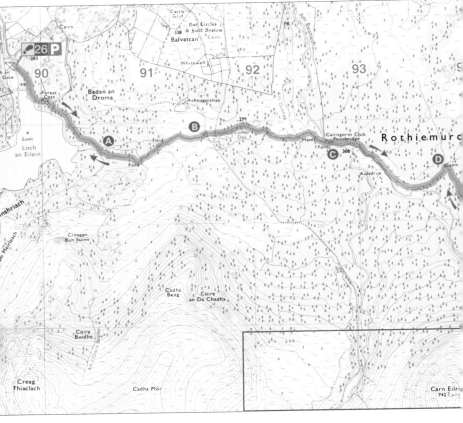

0 200   400   600   800 METRES 1
                                  KILOMETRES
                                  MILES
0   200   400   600 YARDS ½

track from Whitewell comes in from the left here.) The path continues with Lochan Deò on the right.

Keep a look out for the Cairngorm Club Footbridge at **C**, this is 20 yds to the left of our path. Cross the bridge, noting the date the bridge was built, and also the distances and times to various places from this point, and turn right.

At point **D** turn right. The Lairig Ghru path is signposted and marked with a low cairn of boulders, neither of which are too obvious. The path is narrower and rough now as it climbs above the Allt Druidh, which is seen down to the right through the trees.

As the trees thin out a knoll, actually a ridge of

Loch an Eilein and its island castle ruin

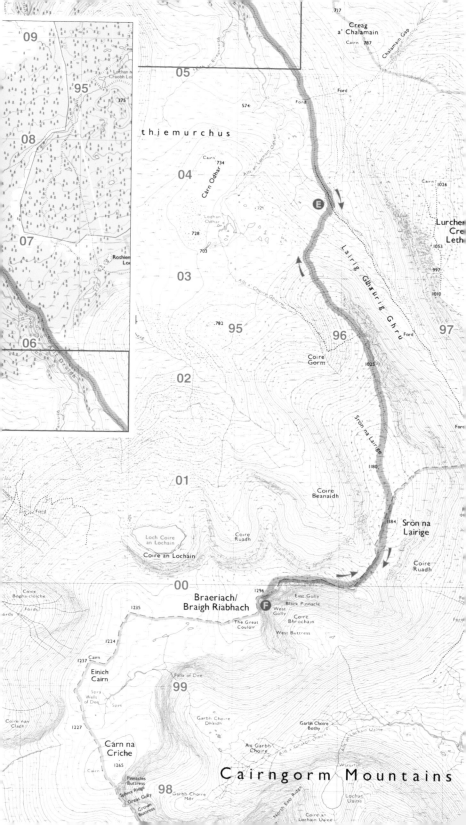

glacial moraine, provides a good stopping place, with views back over the forest to Aviemore and far beyond. As progress is made towards the Lairig Ghru a path joins from the left from Rothiemurchus Lodge.

At **E** the site of the (now demolished) Sinclair Hut is reached. Another path joins from the left, this time from the Chalamain Gap, a glacial overflow. Lurcher's Crag looms high on our left. Turn right, cross the burn and head for the base of Sron na Lairige. After about 300 yds turn left and head up the lower slopes of Sron na Lairige, keeping the steep drop over crags into the Lairig Ghru always on the left. With one eye on the map, head for spot height 1,180m (3,870ft), the ridge broadens into a plateau, then over the summit at spot height 1,184m. Drop down a little to the col between Coire Beabaidh and Coire Ruadh, then ascend the final easy slopes to the summit of Braeriach **F**.

An Garbh Choire lies to the left. It is one of the finest corries in Scotland, being some 1,500 ft (455m) deep to the main river, and about half that depth to the floor of the several upper corries, from the surrounding rim of cliffs.

The most impressive feature visible from the summit is the sheer area of land between 3,000 and 4,000 feet above sea level. Here one can fully appreciate the extent of the Cairngorm plateau and how the Lairig Ghru so dramatically divides it. The return follows the route of ascent all the way back to the car park, with spectacular views over Strathspey being ahead for almost the whole way. ●

Lurcher's Crag from Sron na Lairige

The Lairig Ghru

Start	On the lane from Inverdruie about ¼ mile before Whitewell	**GPS waypoints**
Distance	12¾ miles (20.5km)	🖉 NH 914 090
Height gain	1,705 feet (520m)	Ⓐ NH 916 079
Approximate time	7 hours	Ⓑ NH 938 075
Parking	Layby and verge parking at the start	Ⓒ NH 950 057
		Ⓓ NH 958 037
Ordnance Survey maps	Landranger 36 (Grantown & Aviemore), Explorer OL57 (Cairn Gorm & Aviemore)	Ⓔ NH 974 063

This long walk should only be attempted in good conditions when the higher parts are certain to be clear of snow (which may last into May or even June). *It climbs through the ancient Rothiemurchus pine forest to the rocky pass of Lairig Ghru (which ultimately leads to Braemar). This route turns off the Lairig Ghru shortly before the summit to visit two more spectacular passes – the Chalamain Gap and Eag a' Chait – before returning via Rothiemurchus Lodge. Bad visibility would not only make navigation difficult (though there are few places where the path might be missed) but would also deny you views of some of the best Cairngorm scenery.*

The road to Whitewell provides popular wayside picnic places and is also a convenient starting point for expeditions into the hills.

🖉 Take the vehicle track from the layby, curving to the right and descend to the track coming from Coylumbridge. Turn right here, later passing through a gate and then a kissing-gate in a deer fence to leave the Rothiemurchus Estate. A path leaves to the left soon after this but continue to a crossroads Ⓐ and turn left there.

This path passes the tree-fringed Lochan Deò and wanders through a picturesque part of the ancient Rothiemurchus pine forest before it meets with the Lairig Ghru coming from Coylum Bridge. Bear right here

towards the sound of rushing water and the Cairngorm Club Footbridge, which spans the Am Beanaidh and dates from 1912. Once over the bridge, follow the river upstream past an idyllic shady spot where the Allt Druidh

The Lairig Ghru near the end of the pine forest

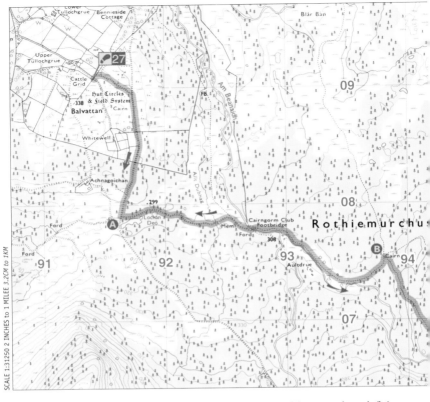

SCALE 1:31250 2 INCHES to 1 MILE 3.2CM to 1KM

0 200 400 600 800 METRES 1
                              KILOMETRES
                              MILES
0   200   400   600 YARDS 1/2

joins it. The path follows this tributary closely at first but then swings left and climbs to a forest crossroads known as Piccadilly **B**. Turn right here to pass the cairn following the sign to Lairig Ghru on a path which climbs gradually through the trees above Allt Druidh. As you climb the Scots pines become smaller and more sparse. Look back for fine views with the buildings of Aviemore just discernible in the distance.

After about an hour you reach the point **C** where a path from Rothiemurchus Lodge joins from the left. From here the going becomes tougher with loose rocks underfoot and a steeper gradient. The path can be seen for a mile or so ahead

climbing steadily towards a cleft in the hills. There is a brief view to the right of the Braeriach corries before they are hidden by the steep slopes which crowd in on the Lairig Ghru. The path runs by the burn once more and crosses **D** another coming up from the Chalamain Gap and continuing on the other side to the summit of Braeriach.

There is an option at **D**. The route is actually to the left here, up the path which climbs between Lurcher's Crag (to the right) and Creag a' Chalamain (to the left). *However, if time and energy allow you may like to go another 2 1/2 miles (4km) up the Lairig Ghru to the crest of the pass and look southwards into Glen Dee.*

From **D** the route continues steeply up a path which has recently been repaired to climb like a staircase for a little way. Look back for a view of the Lairig Ghru under the massive whale-back of Ben Macdui. The path crosses a boggy stretch before climbing again to the boulder-filled Chalamain Gap. Once at the summit of this pass, the path winds ahead towards the mountain road. It descends through more peat bogs; the tree roots are relics of the ancient pine forest. The path ends its gentle descent to climb steeply after crossing a burn. Turn left **E** immediately after this stream on to a path which follows the watercourse. Look left for a view of the Chalamain Gap. Again, as you reach the summit of this pass, Eag a' Chait, progress is slowed by boulders. At the summit there is a tremendous view over Loch Morlich to Aviemore. The next objective,

Rothiemurchus Lodge, can be seen with Loch an Eilein beyond.

The path descends steeply with a fence to the right. The ground is very boggy just before the Lodge and the path ends near the helicopter pad. Follow the roadway to a bell which commemorates the site of the original Rothiemurchus hut. Take the path by the bell past a seat and picnic table, and bear right off the track after the table to follow a sign to Lairig Ghru.

The path, which is often damp underfoot, climbs steadily to **C** with more wonderful views en route. Turn right on to the Lairig Ghru and retrace your steps to the Cairngorm Club Footbridge. Photographers will appreciate the beauty of Lochan Deò, passed just before you turn right **A** to return to the starting point. ●

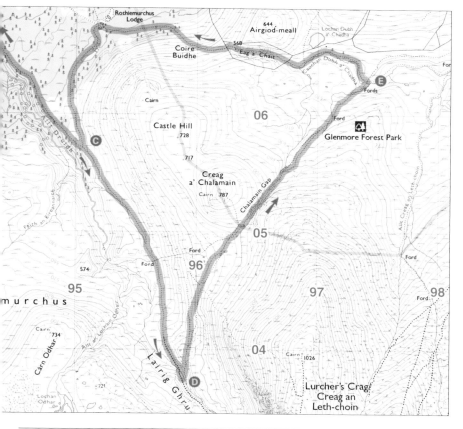

Lochnagar and Loch Muick

		GPS waypoints
Start	Spittal of Glenmuick	
Distance	14 miles (22.4km)	
Height gain	2,790 feet (850m)	
Approximate time	8 hours	
Parking	Car park, at the end of the public road through Glen Muick from Ballater	
Ordnance Survey maps	Landranger 44 (Ballater & Glen Clova), Explorer OL53 (Lochnagar, Glen Muick & Glen Clova)	

GPS waypoints

- 🖉 NO 309 851
- Ⓐ NO 299 858
- Ⓑ NO 273 862
- Ⓒ NO 260 857
- Ⓓ NO 248 852
- Ⓔ NO 275 824

This long walk (including a climb of about 2,000ft/610m) may be shortened by returning along the north-west shore of Loch Muick from Glas-allt-Shiel. Lochnagar is a monarch of mountains even though its summit (3,788ft/1,155m) is modest compared to some neighbours. This is forgotten at the summit, overlooking the grandest of all corries and a landscape that comprises almost half of Scotland. The Lochnagar massif covers 63 sq miles (163 sq km) with 11 tops over 3,000ft (914m). The precipitous drops on its eastern side have claimed many lives so it is very important to have a favourable weather forecast and good outdoor clothing, plus a map and compass.

🖉 Walk from the car park past the information point and turn right following the waymark on to the Lochnagar path. This crosses the river and there is an enticing glimpse of vertical rock faces framed by folds in the hills. When the path comes to the driveway for Allt-na-giubhsaich Ⓐ take the signposted path between the trees (left) and the stable block of the lodge (right), initially following electricity lines to cross a bridge and enter woodland. Allt-na-giubhsaich was used by Queen Victoria as a 'cottage' where she and Prince Albert would come to escape the formalities of life at Balmoral, attended by just a handful of servants.

There is an attractive short length of path which winds through trees before it reaches a Land Rover track which takes the route out of woodland and on to the open hill. Almost 2 miles of straightforward walking follows as the track climbs steadily up to the watershed, passing above the ravine named Clais Rathadan. The top of the col is at 2,224ft (678m) and the track turns north to descend Glen Gelder. However, the Lochnagar route is to the left here Ⓑ, marked by a cairn, on a path which heads westwards. About 80 minutes of walking will bring you to this point.

The well repaired path climbs towards the gap between the conical Meikle Pap on the right and the more irregular Cuidhe Crom on the left. A rectangular block set on top of a boulder to the left of the path may catch your eye. This is a memorial to Bill Stuart who died on Lochnagar on 16 August 1953. It is sited by a spring named the Fox Cairn Well, and you will need to make the most of its waters if the day is warm as this is the last spring passed on the way up.

Continue to the top of the col on a new (2006) section of slabbed footpath. Once over the col  the path continues to the left through a boulder field and the going gets tough. Although the path is faint at first, it improves to rejoin a better path higher up.

The falls on the Glas Allt

Once on top of the summit plateau take the path which leads to the peaks a safe distance from the edge of the corrie – this is well marked by cairns.

The Red Spout is a point where the rocky edge ends and a funnel of red earth seems to lead directly down to the loch about 600ft (183m) below. Certainly on this initial stretch of the plateau it is important to stay away from the edge, if only to make certain of where the return path leaves. There is a short stretch where the path climbs through a narrow, rocky defile. The homeward path leaves south eastwards immediately after this ⒹD and you can see it below following the course of the Glas Allt, a small burn at first but a more substantial stream later when it plunges down to Loch Muick.

The path becomes broader after ⒹD and soon reaches Cac Carn Mor where there is a large cairn. However, this is not the summit even though the cliffs here give breathtaking views of the corrie. The true summit is about ¼ mile farther on to the north-west, a rocky tor capped by a trig point and a mountain indicator

dating from 1924. This is Cac Carn Beag, which confusingly (and politely) translates as 'the cairn of the little heap of manure'. The mountain indicator (which is ceramic) shows points from Ben Nevis and Ben Lomond, to the Caithness and Pentland Hills. On a really clear day you can see The Cheviot whose ridge forms the border with England. However, the chief impression is of wilderness where there are few features recognisable as being the works of man.

Lochnagar has inspired many writers including Lord Byron. References abound in his work and his *Lachin y Gair* ends:

'England! Thy beauties are tame
  and domestic
To one who has roved o'er the
  mountains afar!
Oh, for the crags that are wild and
  majestic!
The steep frowning glories of dark
  Loch na Garr.'

Once you have enjoyed the view from here, return to ⒹD and instead of turning left go straight ahead on the twisting path down towards the Glas

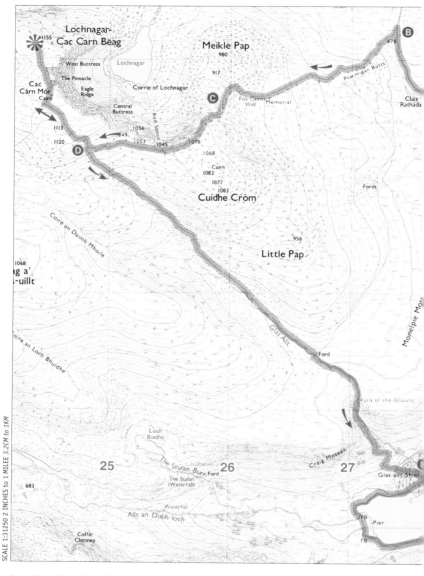

Lochnagar-
Cac Carn Beag

West Buttress

The Pinnacle

Cac
Carn Mòr
Cairn

Eagle
Ridge

Lochnagar

Corrie of Lochnagar

Central
Buttress

Red Spout

1056

1049

1120

1045

1078

.1068

Cairn
1082

1077

1083

Cuidhe Cròm

Meikle Pap
980

917

Fox Cairn
Well

Memorial

956

Little Pap

Clais
Rathada

Ptarmigan Butts

Monelpie Mo

Fords

Corrie an Daimh Mhoile

1068
g a'
-uillt

oire an Loch Bhuidhe

Glas Allt

Ford

Falls of the Glasallt

Loch
Buidhe

The Stulan Burn Ford

The Stulan
(Waterfall)

Waterfall

Allt an Dubh-loch

Craig Moseen

Glas-allt-Shiel

683

25

26

27

Coffin
Chimney

FB

Pier

FB

SCALE 1:31250 2 INCHES to 1 MILE 3.2CM to 1KM

0   200   400   600   800 METRES 1
                            KILOMETRES
                            MILES
0   200   400   600 YARDS   ½

Allt ('the green burn'). The dark cliffs above Loch Muick can be seen ahead but there is no sight of the loch itself. The path crosses to the south-west bank of the burn over a wooden footbridge and a delightful part of the descent follows with the stream close to the left. Soon there are small

cataracts – forerunners of the Glas Allt Falls – and Loch Muick comes into view. The main waterfall has a drop of about 70ft and is well seen from the narrow path.

When the path reaches the woods which surround Glas-allt-Shiel go through the old stone wall and continue downhill on the path to reach the house **E**. If you are tired at this point then turn left onto the

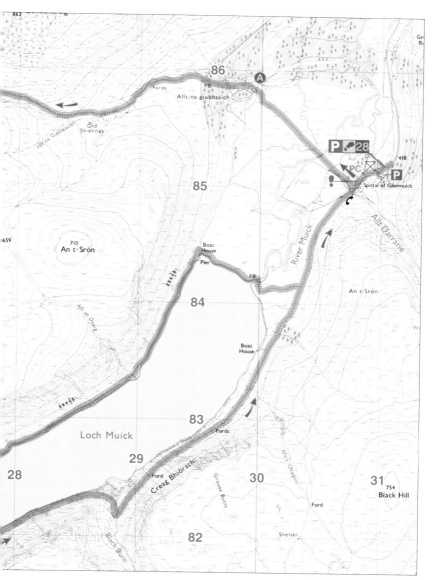

drive and follow it along the north-west shore of the loch. Then turn right by a boathouse at the lower end of the loch on to a good path which leads to the popular lochside path from the information centre.

The longer route entails going round the top end of Loch Muick to reach the path seen earlier following the shoreline. Turn right and follow the waymarkers to reach the lochside

path. A 3½-mile (5.5km) walk back to the Spittal of Glenmuick from this point is constantly delightful, the scenery encompassing views across the loch with Creag a' Ghlas-uillt occasionally seen above the steep slopes facing the loch. After crossing the Black Burn the views back are stunning in the evening light and make a grand finale to a memorable day on the hills. ●

Further Information

 Walkers and the Law

Walkers in Scotland have long enjoyed a moral and de facto right of access. Nothing much has changed except that this is now enshrined in *The Land Reform (Scotland) Act 2003*. The Act tells you where you have right of access and *The Scottish Outdoor Access Code* sets out your responsibilities when exercising your rights. These rights came into effect on 9 February 2005.

Walkers following the routes in this book should not have any problems but it is as well to know something about the law as it affects access, particularly as the legislation in Scotland is significantly different from elsewhere in Britain. Mostly, though, it's just common sense. Be considerate to other land users, look after the places you visit and take responsibility for your own safety.

The Scottish Outdoor Access Code

1. Take responsibility for your own actions.
2. Respect people's privacy and peace of mind. When close to a house or garden, keep a sensible distance from the house, use a path or track if there is one, and take extra care at night.
3. Help land managers and others to work safely and effectively. Do not hinder land management operations and follow advice from land managers. Respect requests for reasonable limitations on when and where you can go.
4. Care for your environment. Do not disturb wildlife, leave the environment as you find it and follow a path or track if there is one.
5. Keep your dog under proper control. Do not take it through fields of calves and lambs, and dispose of dog dirt.
6. Take extra care if you are organising an event or running a business and ask the landowner's advice.

Some fairly comprehensive guidance is available at:
www.outdooraccess-scotland.com

The following covers some of the most common situations affecting walkers.

Car Parking

Motorised vehicles are not included in the access rights, but most people will use a vehicle to reach the start of a walk. It's important to park sensibly and avoid causing an obstruction. Use a car park if one is nearby. If not, make sure you do not block the entrance to a field or building, make it difficult for other road users or damage the verge.

Dogs

Dog walkers are covered by the legislation provided they keep their dogs under control at all times. Avoid fields with sheep during the lambing season (spring). During the bird-breeding season (April – July) keep your dog on a lead while near breeding habitats. Where crossing fields containing animals keep your dog on a short lead.

Farm Steadings

There is no legal right of access to farm steadings. In practice though many tracks and paths do go through farm steadings and you should consider the following advice:

If a right of way or core path goes through the steading then you can follow that.

If an alternative route has been signposted round the steading then it should be used.

If the route through the steading has been taken on a customary basis you may be able to continue to do so.

You may go through the steading if the farmer gives you permission.

Otherwise you will have to exercise your legal right to go around the farm steading and buildings.

Whatever route you use through, or

round, a farm steading exercise care, avoid machinery and livestock and respect the privacy of people living on the farm.

Fields
Keep to paths where possible or walk around the margins of a field under crops. Bear in mind that grass is also grown as a crop. Where fields have been sprayed there are occasions when the landowner has a responsibility to keep people out for health and safety reasons for anything from a few hours to three or four days. Obey any signs or advice from the landowner and work out an alternative route, perhaps through an adjacent field.

Golf Courses
You have a right of access to cross golf courses, but must avoid damage to the playing surface and never step onto the greens. Cross as quickly as possible but consider the rights of the players at the same time. Wait for players to play their shot before crossing the fairway; if you're close to someone about to play, stop and stand still. Keep to any paths that exist and keep dogs on a short lead.

Deer Stalking
During the hunting season walkers should check to ensure that the walks they are planning avoid deer stalking operations.

Culling is an essential part of the management of a sustainable deer population and to avoid overgrazing and damage to fragile habitats.

The red stag stalking season is from 1 July to 20 October, hinds are culled from 21 October to 15 February. September and October tend to be the busiest months. The roe buck stalking season is from 1 April to 20 October, with June to August seeing the peak of activity. The doe-stalking season is from 21 October to 31 March.

During the busy periods of the season stalking can take place six days of the week but never on a Sunday.

The easiest way to find out if the walk you are planning is affected is to refer to

the Hillphones website www.snh.org.uk/hillphones. Here you can find a map of the phones and the relevant numbers. Calls are charged at normal rates and you will hear a recorded message that is changed each morning.

Grouse Shooting
The season runs from 12 August to 10 December. During this period please follow any advice regarding alternative routes on grouse moors to minimise disturbance to the shoot. Avoid crossing land where a shoot is in progress until it is absolutely safe to do so.

 ## Global Positioning System (GPS)
What is GPS?
GPS is a worldwide radio navigation system that uses a network of 24 satellites and receivers, usually hand-held, to calculate positions. By measuring the time it takes a signal to reach the receiver, the distance from the satellite can be estimated. Repeat this with several satellites and the receiver can then use triangulation to establish the position of the receiver.

How to use GPS with Ordnance Survey mapping
Each of the walks in this book includes GPS co-ordinate data that reflects the walk position points on Ordnance Survey maps.

GPS and OS maps use different models for the earth and co-ordinate systems, so when you are trying to relate your GPS position to features on the map the two will differ slightly. This is especially the case with height, as the model that relates the GPS global co-ordinate system to height above sea level is very poor.

When using GPS with OS mapping, some distortion – up to 16ft (5m) – will always be present. Moreover, individual features on maps may have been surveyed only to an accuracy of 23ft (7m) (for 1:25000 scale maps), while other features, e.g. boulders, are usually only shown schematically.

In practice, this should not cause undue difficulty, as you will be near enough to your objective to be able to spot it.

How to use the GPS data in this book
There are various ways you can use the GPS data in this book.

1. Follow the route description while checking your position on your receiver when you are approaching a position point.

2. You can also use the positioning information on your receiver to verify where you are on the map.

3. Alternatively, you can use some of the proprietary software that is available. At the simple end there is inexpensive software, which lets you input the walk positions (waypoints), download them to the gps unit and then use them to assist your navigation on the walks.

At the upper end of the market Ordnance Survey maps are available in electronic form. Most come with software that enables you to enter your walking route onto the map, download it to your gps unit and use it, alongside the route description, to follow the route.

Visitors and the Mountain Environment – a note from the RSPB

The high Cairngorms are outstandingly important for the extent and variety of their habitats and associated flora and fauna. It is now widely accepted that some of the high level routes described in this guide cross areas where the soils and vegetation are especially fragile. Here, even relatively modest use of the ground by people can lead to damage. The severe climate and thin infertile soils mean that recovery of damaged areas will be very slow and uncertain. The large number of people who visit Cairn Gorm and the wider mountain area, encouraged by the easy access

provided by the ski road, car park and chairlift, has resulted in extensive loss of soils and vegetation.

In part as a response to these pressures a wide range of landowners and special interest groups have formed the Cairn Gorm Tourism Management Programme.

A number of management principles have been defined. The key one, in the context of this guide book, is that numbers of visitors reaching the summit of Cairn Gorm should not increase beyond current levels and that on the plateau between Cairn Gorm and Ben Macdui, and in the northern corries, numbers should be reduced. The aim is to prevent further damage to habitats and to allow for sustained recovery.

Targets for the level of reductions and mechanisms to achieve them have yet to be agreed. However, the Tourism Management Programme Group intends that visitor management initiatives will be implemented over the coming years. In the mean time, when walking the high level routes suggested in this guide, please endeavour to heed the Cairngorm Code.

Cairngorm Code

Avoid disturbing wildlife:
- go quietly so you do not disturb birds and animals
- do not pick any flowers or plants
- try to keep to well marked paths
- if your dog is with you keep it close to you

Leave the mountain undamaged:
- do not go higher than you need to
- keep to the middle of paths and do not take short cuts
- do not move rocks

Improve the appearance of the Cairngorms:
- take your litter home
- reduce erosion by keeping to paths
- walk in single file so people have room to pass

Look after your own safety:
- remember that storms can blow up

The Chalamain Gap in winter

deteriorate.

Some of the walks in this book venture into remote country and others climb high summits, and these expeditions should only be undertaken in good summer conditions. In winter they could well need the skills and experience of mountaineering rather than walking. In midwinter the hours of daylight are of course much curtailed, but given crisp, clear late-winter days many of the shorter expeditions would be perfectly feasible, if the guidelines given are adhered to.

very suddenly at any time of year
- wear suitable clothes and footwear
- have map and compass with you at all times.

 ## Safety on the Hills

The Highland hills and lower but remote areas call for care and respect. The idyllic landscape of the tourist brochures can change rapidly into a world of gales, rain and mist, potentially lethal for those ill-equipped or lacking navigational skills. The Scottish hills in winter can be arctic in severity, and even in summer, snow can lash the summits.

At the very least carry adequate wind- and waterproof outer garments, food and drink to spare, a basic first-aid kit, whistle, map and compass – and know how to use them. Wear boots. Plan within your capabilities. If going alone ensure you leave details of your proposed route. Heed local advice, listen to weather forecasts, and do not hesitate to modify plans if conditions

Mountain Rescue

In case of emergency the standard procedure is to dial 999 and ask for the police who will assess and deal with the situation.

First, however, render first aid as required and make sure the casualty is made warm and comfortable. The distress signal (six flashes/whistle-blasts, repeated at minute intervals) may bring help from other walkers in the area. Write down essential details: exact location (six-figure reference), time of accident, numbers involved, details of injuries, steps already taken; then despatch a messenger to phone the police.

If leaving the casualty alone, mark the site with an eye-catching object. Be patient; waiting for help can seem interminable.

 ## Useful Organisations

Association for the Protection of Rural Scotland
Dolphin House, 4 Hunter Square,

Edinburgh, EH1 1QW
Tel. 0131 225 7012
www.aprs.scot

Cairngorms National Park
14 The Square, Grantown-on-Spey
PH26 3HG
Tel. 01479 873535
www.cairngorms.co.uk

Camping and Caravan Club
Greenfields House, Westwood Way,
Coventry CV4 8JH
Tel. 024 7647 5426
www.campingandcaravanningclub.co.uk

Forestry Commission Scotland
Silvan House, 231 Corstorphine Road,
Edinburgh EH12 7AT

 ## Glossary of Gaelic Names

Most of the place names in this region are Gaelic in origin, and this list gives some of the more common elements, which will allow readers to understand otherwise meaningless words and appreciate the relationship between place names and landscape features. Place names often have variant spellings, and the more common of these are given here.

aber	mouth of loch, river
abhainn	river
allt	stream
auch, ach	field
bal, bail, baile	town, homestead
bàn	white, fair, pale
bealach	hill pass
beg, beag	small
ben, beinn	hill
bhuidhe	yellow
blar	plain
brae, braigh	upper slope, steepening
breac	speckled
cairn	pile of stones, often marking a summit
cam	crooked
càrn	cairn, cairn-shaped hill
caol, kyle	strait
ceann, ken, kin	head
cil, kil	church, cell
clach	stone
clachan	small village
cnoc	hill, knoll, knock
coille, killie	wood
corrie, coire, choire	mountain hollow
craig, creag	cliff, crag
crannog, crannag	man-made island
dàl, dail	field, flat
damh	stag
dearg	red
druim, drum	long ridge
dubh, dhu	black, dark
dùn	hill fort
eas	waterfall
eilean	island
eilidh	hind
eòin, eun	bird
fionn	white
fraoch	heather
gabhar, ghabhar, gobhar	goat
garbh	rough
geal	white
ghlas, glas	grey
gleann, glen	narrow, valley
gorm	blue, green
inbhir, inver	confluence
inch, inis, innis	island, meadow by river
lag, laggan	hollow
làrach	old site
làirig	pass
leac	slab
liath	grey
loch	lake
lochan	small loch
màm	pass, rise
maol	bald-shaped top
monadh	upland, moor
mór, mor(e)	big
odhar, odhair	dun-coloured
rhu, rubha	point
ruadh	red, brown
sgòr, sgòrr, sgùrr	pointed
sron	nose
stob	pointed
strath	valley (broader than glen)
tarsuinn	traverse, across
tom	hillock (rounded)
tòrr	hillock (more rugged)
tulloch, tulach	knoll
uisge	water, river

Tel. 0300 067 6156
www.scotland.forestry.go.uk

Historic Scotland
Longmore House, Salisbury Place,
Edinburgh EH9 1SH
Tel. 0131 668 8600
www.historic-scotland.gov.uk

Mountaineering Council of Scotland
The Old Granary,
West Mill Street,
Perth PH1 5QP
Tel. 01738 493942
www.mcofs.org.uk

National Trust for Scotland
Hermiston Quay, 5 Cultins Road,
Edinburgh EH11 4DF
Tel. 0131 458 0200
www.nts.org.uk

Ordnance Survey
Tel. 03456 05 05 05
www.ordnancesurvey.co.uk

Ramblers Scotland
Caledonia House, 1 Redheughs Rigg,
South Gyle, Edinburgh, EH12 9DQ
Tel. 0131 472 7006
www.ramblers.org.uk/scotland

Scottish Natural Heritage
Great Glen House, Leachkin Road,
Inverness IV3 8NW
Tel. 01463 725000
www.snh.gov.uk

Grantown-on-Spey: 01479 872478
Newtonmore: 01540 670066
Tomintoul: 01807 580285

Weather forecasts:
Mountain Weather Information Service
www.mwis.org.uk

Ordnance Survey Maps of the Cairngorms

The walks described in this guide are covered by Ordnance Survey 1:50,000 scale (1¼ inches to 1 mile or 2cm to 1km) Landranger map sheets 35, 36, 37, 43, 44, 52.

These all-purpose maps are packed with information to help you explore the area. Viewpoints, picnic sites, places of interest and caravan and camping sites are shown, as well as public rights of way information such as footpaths and bridleways.

To examine this area in more detail, especially if you are planning walks, the Ordnance Survey Explorer maps at 1:25 000 scale (2½ inches to 1 mile or 4cm to 1km) are ideal:

OL51 Atholl
OL52 Glen Shee & Braemar
OL53 Lochnagar, Glen Muick &
    Glen Clova
OL54 Glen Esk & Glen Tanar
OL56 Badenoch & Upper Strathspey
OL57 Cairn Gorm & Aviemore
OL58 Braemar, Tomintoul, Glen Avon
OL59 Aboyne, Alford & Strathdon
OL60 Lochindorb, Grantown-on-Spey
    & Carrbridge
OL61 Grantown-on-Spey & Hills of
    Cromdale

Ordnance Survey maps and guides are available from most booksellers, stationers and newsagents.

Further Information

Ordnance Survey

Pathfinder®Guides

Britain's best-loved walking guides